Thoughts for Young Mothers

By Elsie D. Holsinger

MOODY PRESS
CHICAGO

Printed in the United States of America

Thoughts for Young Mothers

Preface

The joy and responsibility of motherhood has been assigned to young women many of whom have had no previous experience or training in the rearing of children.

A child is like a delicate camellia whose petals are marred by thoughtless handling. This little book gives suggestions on the handling of little lives which are far more delicate and valuable than camellias. Encouragement from my own bouquet of blossoming youth has spurred on the preparation of this book.

Sitting under my husband's ministry for many years has enriched my knowledge of the Scriptures, without which this volume would have little value.

Who can find a virtuous woman? for her price is far above rubies.—Proverbs 31:10

A prudent wife is from the Lord.—Proverbs 19:14

Lo, children are an heritage of the Lord.—Psalm 127:3

Contents

Living to Win

That I may win Christ, and be found in him, not having mine own righteousness, which is of the law, but that which is through the faith of Christ, the righteousness which is of God by faith.—Philippians 3:8, 9

LAST NIGHT I was weary with the duties and activities of the day. When I lay down at last, it was a relief to lie between the cool sheets and think of nothing—absolutely nothing. I was too tired to relive the day that had just closed. I didn't have the energy to plan for tomorrow. "For so he giveth his beloved sleep." What a blessing from the Lord, an uninterrupted, restful, refreshing sleep! "He knoweth our frame, he remembereth that we are dust. Like as a father pitieth his children, so the Lord pitieth them that fear him, and delivereth them." I repeated these comforting Bible verses as I dozed off into restful slumber.

The bright morning sun streamed into the room. It was morning in my heart! Gone was the weariness of mind and body. A new day, a new adventure for Christ, was beginning.

"This one thing I do, forgetting those things which are behind, and reaching forth unto those things which are before, I press toward the mark for the prize of the high calling of God in Christ Jesus." If I am to win Christ, I must make the gaining of Him my one ambition.

I had a little talk with Jesus before the cheery voices of my family called, "Mother." How I love their familiar voices! Each child laughs and talks as he wakens. I thank God for each one of them. He has given them to me to bring them up for Him. He created each precious personality. He has redeemed each one and knows him by name.

How warm and comfortable the sun felt as it streamed through the kitchen window! I thanked the Lord for this south exposure. Suppose I were cooking breakfast in a chilly room facing the north. It might be rather depressing and dull.

It is such a joy to see the children sitting around the table, hungry and happy. Everything tastes so good to them. Their cheeks are glowing pink with health. Their little bodies are strong and sturdy. I can almost see them grow. I read them a verse or two from the Bible after they finish eating their bowls of hot cereal. Their souls must have food as well as their bodies. When they have finished their breakfast, we can read together and I can have their undivided attention. They must listen reverently because God is talking.

Let Christ be the light of your home. Let Him take the burden of your work. Christ will make it really worth while to cook and sew, to wash and mend. Every child of God is in full-time service for Him. So take heart, Mother; He knows, He sees, He cares!

Are your children still pre-schoolers? Do you sigh each morning and say, "How many more years of this daily drudgery do I have to endure?" Remember, your life as a mother can be a glorious adventure. Start your home with Christ as its foundation. Keep in your heart that song of victory, "Thanks be unto God who always causeth us to triumph in Christ" (II Cor. 2:14).

Love, peace, gentleness, sympathy, and understanding are the unseen qualities which truly make your home. The furniture and accessories of a house do not necessarily constitute a home. You, Mother, make the home. *House* and *home* have very different meanings. A house has four outside walls and many rooms. A home may consist of only one room. Homes have more to them than walls and roof; the components of a real home are warmth of spirit and joy in the Lord.

I know a little home that is small and unfinished. There are no running water and plumbing facilities. The father brings water home each evening in ten-gallon cans. There is a joyful mother in this home. God has blessed the young parents with three little ones. The mother is even the envy of an unmarried girl who has everything but happiness! The true elements of a home cannot be seen with the physical eyes. The Christian spirit of a home can be sensed as one

11

enters the door. Just as sweet perfume pervades a room, so the love of Christ sweetens the conversation and attitude of each one in the family circle.

What are you out to win this morning? Do you have any special ambition in life? You say, "I'm in the midst of rearing my family." I know that, but what is your ambition for each of your children? Do you want your child to be the best-dressed in the school? Or do you want him to be the most popular among his classmates? Perhaps you want him to have the highest marks and be the "brain" of the class? But here is an ambition that "tops" them all. Paul the apostle put it this way: "That I may win Christ!" So, make this your motto, not only in your own life but in your children's lives. Ask the Lord to give you strength, and then bend all your efforts toward accomplishing this end.

Costume Jewelry

That our daughters may be as corner stones, polished after the similitude of a palace.—Psalm 144:12b

I WANT TO TELL you about a wonderful verse that is found in God's Word. Every woman has a desire in her heart to be beautiful. The Lord understood this when He told us that our adorning should "not be that outward adorning of plaiting of the hair, and wearing of gold, or of putting on of apparel; but let it be the hidden man of the heart, in that which is not corruptible, even the ornament of a meek and quiet spirit, which is in the sight of God of great price." True beauty originates in the heart. There is a light and sweetness in the true Christian mother's face which the world desires but cannot obtain.

The daily papers are full of beauty hints. They suggest means or external remedies to make you attractive. But God's prescription of beauty is especially prepared for the heart. The ornament of a meek and quiet spirit adorns your inner being. Its luster is so bright that it is reflected in your facial expression. This ornament is a gift of God.

It is good to hear some member of the family say, "Mother, you're beautiful." Maybe your features are not so pretty. Perhaps you have often looked in the mirror and shaken your head in despair. Why, then, are you beautiful to your husband and children? It is because of the sweet expression which God has given you. Calmness and love are indelibly stamped on the lines of your face.

Christ wants to transform your heart and make it like His own—patient, long-suffering, loving. He wants to take out of your heart the harshness, irritability, impatience, and critical attitude toward those you love. God has told you how to be beautiful at all times. He wants you to be adorned with an inward peace.

Too often, perhaps, you talk to your family with a note of irritation in your voice. The love of Christ can be shown even in the tone of your voice. If you speak quietly to your family, they will respond quietly. If you shriek at them, they will shout back at you. Your home can be a bedlam or it can be a little bit of heaven. Quiet restfulness in a household is the result of the wearing of this ornament of a meek and quiet spirit. It is important for a happy home. It is found in a Christian mother's heart. God wants to adorn our lives with the beauty of His grace in our hearts. A calm attitude and a quiet voice are unusual traits in most homes. Can you be patient as you answer countless childish questions and respond to numberless requests for help?

The telephone rings, the door-bell chimes, and then the youngest child falls down, screaming. The mother wonders which to attend to first. If she can keep calm during such a stormy session in her home, she is a testimony to the grace of God abounding in her heart. "In quietness and in confidence shall be your strength."

The ornament of a meek and quiet spirit never grows dim with wear. The longer it is worn, the brighter it sparkles. It is incorruptible. Time cannot destroy it. Gold and silver jewels tarnish and wear thin. Other ornaments are lost and stolen. But this ornament of a meek and quiet spirit is not subject to temporal changes. It is a trophy of a life surrendered to the will of your Lord and Saviour Jesus Christ.

Best of all, this ornament is of great price in God's estimation. If God values it highly, we should value it highly also. The heavenly standard should be our standard. May we "adorn the doctrine of God our Saviour in all things."

A Contented Mother

I have learned in whatsoever state I am, therewith to be content.—Philippians 4:11

YOU AND I LIVE just a day at a time, so let us ask God to make this day the very best one in our lives so far. Desire that the Holy Spirit will direct your meditations so that you will appreciate more deeply the salvation that Christ Jesus has provided for you. When we have our eyes constantly on the Lord, the small daily annoyances will mean very little.

"Godliness with contentment is great gain." Our spiritual "uplook" will brighten up our most irksome tasks; otherwise, ordinary housework would become drudgery.

We Christian mothers are more than cooks and housekeepers. We are children of God and joint heirs with Christ. We are His representatives, His ambassadors. God has given us our home with our children as a special place to serve Him. Glorify and praise the Lord just where you are. Ask the Holy Spirit to lead you in the way of the Lord. "He that hath begun a good work in you will perfect it unto the day of Christ" (Phil. 1:6). Be contented and happy!

Perhaps from your dining room window you can see

15

the sunshine casting lights and shadows on shrubs and trees in a garden. There are such exquisite wonders in God's creation. "All things were made by him, and without him was not anything made that was made." The Holy Spirit will open your eyes to see the natural beauties surrounding you when you are contented. You discover the grandeur of the mighty things which God has made. You also realize the delicate beauties of little things which are equally marvelous. Have you ever looked into the face of a fresh-blooming, vari-colored pansy? The snowflake also and the sunbeam can captivate your wonder. Then there are the mountains, hills, and valleys which reveal the wonders of God's creation. David said: "The heavens declare the glory of God, and the firmament showeth his handi-work" (Ps. 19:11).

A contented mother can appreciate all these divinely created surroundings. She can praise the Lord for all His mighty works. Discontent clouds the vision. It hinders the soul in beholding the evidences of God's presence.

Your environment will always be beautiful when Christ is the center of your thoughts and the theme of your thanksgiving. "And be content with such things as ye have, for he hath said, I will never leave thee nor forsake thee, so that we may boldly say, The Lord is my helper, and I will not fear what man can do unto me" (Heb. 13:5).

Perhaps you are in a state of weakness. Praise the

Lord anyway! "For which cause we faint not; but though our outward man perish, yet the inward man is renewed day by day" (II Cor. 4:16). Begin to rejoice in the Lord and you will find "the joy of the Lord is your strength."

Discontent is a bad habit, but contentment can become a habit, too. Everything that God allows to come into life can draw us closer to Him. "All things work together for good to them that love God." Worship Him thankfully and in utter dependence. Trust Him in each unexpected crisis that arises.

Are you in the midst of great perplexity, or do you face an apparently insolvable problem? Do not complain. "With God nothing shall be impossible." Keep looking up unto Jesus your Saviour for strength and wisdom. He has promised to give it to you. Ask Him for guidance and trust Him implicitly.

The following verse is an excellent individual blueprint for every mother's life: "I have learned in whatsoever state I am, therewith to be content."

We mothers have a twenty-four-hour-working day. We have no time off, and we have a permanent job for at least twenty years. Remember the Lord is by your side, ever ready to help you in this almost overwhelming task. "I have set the Lord always before me: because he is at my right hand, I shall not be moved" (Ps. 16:8). You will be contented when you cast all your care upon Him.

Be contented not only with your God-given place

17

but also be satisfied with many or few things that are yours. "A man's life consisteth not in the abundance of the things which he possesseth" (Luke 12:15). Envy and jealousy of others' belongings are sins which we must ask God to take out of these hearts. They will rob us of contentment.

Every difficult situation in life is a new challenge to faith. "Delight thyself in the Lord, and he shall give thee the desires of thine heart" (Ps. 37:4). You will experience a joyful triumph when the Lord sends His help and His deliverance. "Many are the afflictions of the righteous, but the Lord delivereth him out of them all" (Ps. 34:19). After you have prayed about your problem, stand still and see the salvation of the Lord.

Contentment and thanksgiving go hand-in-hand. This combination will triumphantly conquer complaint and worry. We can then sing, "Take your burden to the Lord and leave it there."

Maybe the house needs cleaning; there is a stack of dirty dishes waiting to be washed; the mending of overalls and play clothes is piling up. Praise the Lord for the opportunity and time that He has given you for so many tasks.

Memorize this verse for everyday living: "The Lord is my strength and my shield; my heart trusteth in him and I am helped: therefore my heart greatly rejoiceth; and with my song will I praise him" (Ps. 28:7).

Spiritual Nourishment

I have esteemed the words of his mouth more than my necessary food.—Job 23:12

CHILDREN REQUIRE SPIRITUAL food as well as a balanced diet for physical growth. You are concerned about giving them the proper amounts of proteins, fats, and carbohydrates. You should be equally conscientious about feeding them the pure Word of God. Children need multiple vitamins to grow strong in body. They also must have spiritual vitamins so that "the inner man may be renewed day by day" (II Cor. 4:16).

Jeremiah said, "Thy words were found, and I did eat them; and thy word was . . . the joy and rejoicing of my heart" (Jer. 15:16). You too must "eat" the Word of God each day if you are to be strong in the Lord. The Holy Spirit uses the word *eat* to teach us the importance of bringing the Bible instruction to bear in our daily actions. It is good to memorize a wonderful promise and then live by it. Put it into practice as you perform your household tasks. Tell your children about it so that they too can assimilate the Word of God into their lives. Jesus said, "Feed my lambs" (John 21:15). God has given you some precious lambs for His flock. You are to nurture them in the Word of God. Strive to feed them God's Word every day. "How sweet are thy words unto my taste! yea, sweeter than honey to my mouth!" (Ps. 119:103).

19

"Desire the sincere milk of the Word that ye may grow thereby'" (I Peter 2:2). You see that the Christian must grow in the Lord, and to do this he must feed upon the Holy Scriptures. "O taste and see that the Lord is good; blessed is the man that trusteth in him" (Ps. 34:8).

You can read the Old Testament stories to your children and they will love them. These narratives will be food for their souls. "Now all these things happened unto them for examples: and they are written for our admonition" (I Cor. 10:11).

Just as we mix certain foods together for added nourishment, so we must mix faith with each verse that we read. It is written of some listeners that "the word did not profit them, not being mixed with faith by them that heard it" (Heb. 4:2). God places a priority on faith: "Without faith it is impossible to please him." And everyone can possess faith: "faith cometh by hearing, and hearing by the Word of God" (Rom. 10:17).

The best time and place for you to feed your children this heavenly manna is at family worship. They must have a daily portion of God's truth if their spiritual stature is to keep up with their physical growth.

We desire our children to grow like little Samuel. "And the child Samuel grew on, and was in favor both with the Lord and with men" (I Sam. 2:26). It was said of our Lord Jesus in His youth: "Jesus increased in wisdom and stature, and in favor with God and man." Here is a fourfold, symmetrical development: Our Lord grew mentally, physically, spiritually, and socially. He is the divine pattern and the example of a perfect development.

Plan to have your family worship immediately after breakfast, before it is time to go to school. You will discover that your children will love this quiet pause in the day's activities. They will look forward to it with pleasure and remind you of it each morning. *Determine* to hold the family altar daily. Perhaps your husband has to go to work before the others in the family awaken. Then, mothers, it is your God-given privilege to conduct the morning devotions.

Perhaps you will want to begin with a Psalm. Read it correctly and distinctly. It will grow to be music to the ears of your family. The Word of God becomes part of their thinking as they hear it every day. Through the years, the familiar ring of the verses will be like heavenly harmony.

It is said in the Book of Nehemiah, concerning those who read God's Word: "So they read in the book in the law of God distinctly, and gave the sense, and caused them to understand the meaning" (Neh. 8:8). Explain the difficult words to your children and ask the Lord to help you make the lessons clear to their young minds. Five minutes is long enough to spend in reading.

As the children's love for Bible stories increases, they will clamor for mother to continue. They will be so interested that they will sigh when the story is ended and the Bible is closed. When you kneel to pray with your children, thank the Lord for His abundant blessings. Ask Him to watch over and prosper Daddy in his daily task. Tell Him you are trusting Him to protect your children from sin and evil, as well as from bodily harm. Ask Him to place a hedge of protection round about every member of the family.

Perhaps you will sometimes end your prayer with these two Scripture verses: "Create in me a clean heart, O God, and renew a right spirit within me . . ." (Ps. 51:10) . "Let the words of my mouth and the meditations of my heart be acceptable in thy sight, O Lord, my strength and my redeemer" (Ps. 19:14) . The children will soon be repeating these closing petitions. They will unconsciously learn the Word of God and hide it in their hearts.

As you return to washing the breakfast dishes and straightening up the house, what a wonderful comfort it is to remember this promise: "The angel of the Lord encampeth round about them that fear him, and delivereth them" (Ps. 34:7) .

"Just one little life to live, so today I will pray that each word and act of mine may reflect the Christ divine whom I love."

Our Thoughts

How precious also are thy thoughts unto me, O God! how great is the sum of them!—Psalm 139:17

WE HAVE LEARNED THAT our thoughts control our actions. This is not a recent discovery, as some would have you suppose. In Proverbs it was written long ago, "As a man thinketh in his heart so is he" (23:7).

What do we mothers think about all day long? During our waking hours our minds are continually active. We think while we work. A mother's day is often a continuous program of action. The only time she can sit down is during a meal. This is often interrupted by frequent trips to the kitchen or to the refrigerator. She thinks on her feet.

Some mothers think only of anticipated pleasures for themselves. Other mothers have their minds completely occupied with the dress they wish they had, or the longed-for luxuries that they cannot afford on their husband's inadequate salary. Such mothers are discontented and unhappy.

A Christian mother thinks of others. She ponders how to develop the sweetest and best disposition in each child that God has given her. She concludes that tact and patience are indispensable. She prays for guidance and wisdom in child-training as she straightens up her home. "If any of you lack wisdom, let him ask of God who giveth to all men liberally, and upbraideth not" (James 1:5). It is good to know that "the fear of the Lord, that is wisdom; and to depart from evil is understanding" (Job 28:28).

A mother's thoughts are very important. Happy thoughts make happy mothers and sorrowful thoughts make sad mothers. Children love happiness and laughter. Keep your mind dwelling on "whatsoever things are true, whatsoever things are honest, whatsoever things are just, whatsoever things are pure, whatsoever things are lovely, whatsoever things are of good report, if there be any virtue, and if there be any praise, think on these things" (Phil. 4:8). Memorizing Scripture is the very best way to think God's thoughts. "Be ye holy for I am holy saith the Lord" (I Peter 1:16).

Our thoughts are swayed very, very much by the literature we read and by the entertainment we indulge in. Triangle love affairs, gangland holdups, and murder mysteries in story, radio, and television can drive your children's thoughts away from God. "The Lord knoweth the thoughts of man that they are vanity" (Ps. 94:11). A mother can choose programs and recreation that will edify her child's mind. She should encourage him to think thoughts of good rather than to dwell on evil thoughts and evil deeds. Stories and pictures of robberies and murder will become ordinary and will harden his thoughts against law and order. Interest him in hobbies and handcrafts. Direct his thoughts into healthy, happy channels.

Some mothers are continually living in the past. They allow their minds to be engrossed with previous mistakes which time can never change. Their thoughts

24

are retrospective and introspective. They regret what was said and what was done. They wish that they had made wiser decisions. How different everything would have been if only the actions of yesteryear had been different! These incidents are relived endlessly in the mind. Nothing will sap your mental energy more than regret and remorse. When Satan tempts you with such heartache, remember this comforting advice from Scripture: "Forgetting those things which are behind, and reaching forth unto those things which are before, I press toward the mark for the prize of the high calling of God in Christ Jesus" (Phil. 3:13, 14).

Then there are the sins and imperfections of the past that are a source of accusation and mental distress. Some mothers weepingly confess, "How can I forget the terrible things I have said and done?" God has an answer for that dilemma also: "If we confess our sins, he is faithful and just to forgive us our sins, and to cleanse us from all unrighteousness" (I John 1:9). When God forgives, He forgets; so we should forget too.

> Let the wicked forsake his way, and the unrighteous man his thoughts; and let him return unto the Lord, and he will have mercy upon him; and to our God, for he will abundantly pardon. For my thoughts are not your thoughts, neither are your ways my ways, saith the Lord. For as the heavens are higher than the earth, so are my ways higher than your ways, and my thoughts than your thoughts. (Isa. 55:7, 8).

When Christ is our Saviour we can ask Him to direct our thoughts. Our wild imaginations and evil surmisings will disappear from our minds when the Holy Spirit governs our thinking. "Casting down imaginations, and every evil thing that exalteth itself against the knowledge of God, and bringing into captivity every thought to the obedience of Christ" (II Cor. 10:5). When we open our heart's door to the Saviour He will come in and purify our works and our thoughts. "Commit thy works unto the Lord and thy thoughts shall be established" (Prov. 16:3).

We can ask the Lord to examine our thoughts and purify them. "Search me, O God, and know my heart; try me and know my thoughts and see if there be any wicked way in me, and lead me in the way everlasting" (Ps. 139:23, 24).

How strengthening it is to repeat again and again the Word of God that we have hidden in our hearts! "In the multitude of my thoughts within me thy comforts delight my soul" (Ps. 94:19).

There are many things we should forget, but there are also glorious things which we should remember. "I have remembered thy name, O Lord, in the night, and have kept thy law" (Ps. 119:55).

May this be your prayer: "Let the words of my mouth and the meditation of my heart be acceptable in thy sight, O Lord, my strength and my redeemer."

"Thou God Seest Me"

He that formed the eye, shall he not see?—Psalm
94:9

MANY MOTHERS CHOKE UP with emotion when
they register their youngsters in the first
grade at school. Babyhood is truly at an end
when school begins. From now on your child will become less and less dependent on you. You cannot accompany him everywhere he goes as you have in the
past. This necessary separation compels you to trust
your children to the Lord's care. "Blessed are all they
that put their trust in him" (Ps. 2:12). We can pray
that they will be protected from accident and from
spiritual and moral harm.

You have had the exclusive training and teaching
of your child for the first six years of his life. It has
been your opportunity to choose his companions. You
have planned his recreation. You have selected books
and papers which have fascinated him. You have read
him adventure stories. You have traveled with him
from nursery rhymes up to tales of tall adventure.
You have sat side-by-side on the couch engrossed in
pictures and illustrations. You have satisfied his curi-
osity by answering his countless questions. Gradually
you have been laying the foundation of his character.

You have told him the story of Jesus and His love.
He has heard of His Saviour all through his short life.
You have had the joy of hearing from his own lips that

he has opened his little heart to the Saviour. He trusts the Lord Jesus as his Shepherd. You have taught your child to reverence and believe the Word of God. Now he is leaving your tender care to be under the instruction of others. He will mingle with many different types of children. Some of them will tempt him to do evil. But God watches over him. He is a precious lamb in the Saviour's flock.

"Thou God seest me" (Gen. 16:13). This verse will fortify your child against yielding to temptations. Write it indelibly in his mind, heart, and conscience. It will guard him from willful sin because he knows that God is watching him at all times. "The eyes of the Lord are in every place beholding the evil and the good" (Prov. 15:3).

"Thou God seest me." The truth of this verse will constantly remind him of God's presence. It is like a heavenly refrain or chorus which is easy to memorize. "I will instruct thee and teach thee in the way which thou shalt go; I will guide thee with mine eye" (Ps. 32:8). Darkness and loneliness will not frighten him with this faith in his heart.

"Thou God seest me." The Lord Jesus knows all about each temptation that confronts your child, and He is near if and when he is tempted to steal. He will strengthen him to resist the temptation to lie. He will give him courage to say *No* when he might cheat. The Lord watches where he goes, He sees what he does, He hears what is said even in secret. Our deeds and our actions are all known to Him. We cannot hide from Christ our Redeemer. "If I say, Surely the darkness shall cover me, even the night shall be light about me; yea, the darkness hideth not from thee; but the night shineth as the day: the darkness and the light are both alike to thee" (Ps. 139:11) .

We learn that God has created each one of us for a special work and place in the world; He has a definite plan for each little life. He knows each child individually and by name. It is good to know that we are very precious in His sight. "He that keepeth thee will not slumber" (Ps. 121:3) . "For the eyes of the Lord run to and fro throughout the whole earth to show himself strong in behalf of them whose heart is perfect toward him" (II Chron. 16:9) .

When we receive the Lord Jesus as our Saviour, He promises to keep us as the apple of His eye. We are so safe in His wonderful care. "Behold the eye of the Lord is upon them that fear him, upon them that hope in his mercy" (Ps. 33:18) .

"Thou God seest me." When you read this verse over to yourself, emphasize that last little word "me." Individually we are important to the Lord. The Communists teach that we are insignificant as individuals and that we must function collectively, without personal recognition. The Lord Jesus teaches the contrary. During His earthly ministry He was particularly concerned with the welfare of the individual. He helped each one in his particular need. He noticed even the little children and blessed them as they came to Him. All Christ's invitations are to the individual and not simply to the masses. "Come unto me all ye that labor and are heavy laden, and I will give you rest" (Matt. 11:28).

"Thou God seest me." This verse will impart to your child the knowledge that God knows and sees everyone, everywhere, at all times. This truth is a priceless heritage. "For his eyes are upon the ways of man, and he seeth all his goings" (Job. 24:21). The Lord looks down deep into our hearts. "His eyes behold, his eyelids try, the children of men" (Ps. 11:4).

"Thou God seest me." Refresh your hearts often by reading Psalm 139 at family worship. It tells in detail the utter impossibility of ever escaping the watchful eye of our Creator. We can lift our voice to Him confidently. "For the eyes of the Lord are over the righteous and his ears are open unto their prayers" (I Peter 3:12). We read again, "He withdraweth not his eyes from the righteous" (Job 36:7).

The Lord knows when we are happy and when we are sorrowful. He sympathizes with us when we are ill or in distress. We can kneel down and pray as David did, "Look upon my affliction and my pain; and forgive all my sins" (Ps. 25:18).

Perhaps we have a friend who is a missionary far away across the seas. The Lord is mindful of the people in other lands and loves them individually too. We are told, "The Lord looketh from heaven, he beholdeth all the sons of men. From the place of his habitation, he looketh upon all the inhabitants of the earth" (Ps. 33:13, 14).

God sees you, but you cannot see God. "Whom having not seen, ye love; in whom, though now ye see him not, yet believing, ye rejoice with joy unspeakable and full of glory" (I Peter 1:8).

Peacemakers

Blessed are the peacemakers for they shall be called the children of God.—Matthew 5:9

WHAT OF TODAY? Are you thankful and happy? Did you retire last night with tense nerves and headache? Did the children quarrel with each other? Then did they tease the baby until you were ready to give up in despair?

Do not be discouraged! Forestall a day of quarreling by talking to your children about being little peacemakers. Add the word *peacemakers* to your prayer at family altar time. Read to them the verse: "Blessed are the peacemakers, for they shall be called the children of God." Explain this to them briefly. Tell them that they live like children of God when they are peacemakers.

The first quarrel that occurs will be the time and place to apply this lesson. We cannot teach children to be peacemakers by rules and regulations. All such lessons must be taught in the midst of an actual experience. Perhaps it is a picture-book the children are disputing over. Mothers, you can say, "Let's see who wants to be the peacemaker and stop this quarrel." One or the other, or perhaps both will assent with a smile. "I'll be the peacemaker," they shout together, and the quarrel is ended.

When settling an argument, be faithful in your judgments and be impartial in your decisions. A child will sense partiality immediately. A mother must be well rested and free from irritability in order to cope wisely with children who are quarreling. Be sure you understand the cause of the quarrel, or the reason for the misunderstanding. If it is a case of willfulness, the quarrelers can kiss each other and be friends again. If it is a matter of selfishness, then the object of contention can be restored to its rightful owner. "Have peace one with another" (Mark 9:50).

During a quarrel neither child desires to give in. The mother can gently take away the toy and tell the child to play with something else for a while. Many valuable lessons in peacemaking will occur every day. A mother must patiently teach, "precept upon precept, line upon line, here a little, and there a little" (Isa. 28:10). As you teach your children to be peacemakers, you will get a blessing in your own heart.

Peacemakers do not say unkind words. Peacemakers do not grab and fight. Peacemakers dislike strife. Peacemakers desire to be Christlike, because the Lord Jesus Himself was a peacemaker. He made the troubled sea still and calmed anxious hearts. He said: "My peace I give unto you; let not your heart be troubled" (John 14:27). He also said: "These things I have spoken unto you that in me ye might have peace" (John 16:33).

Each child has to be taught to share goodies and playthings with others. There is nothing so conducive to selfishness as to allow a child to eat his apple, or popcorn, or candy while playing with other children. It is good to put this special treat aside for another time, or have him divide it with each child present. Sharing soon becomes a happy habit to a little child. It is one phase of being a peacemaker. This is one secret of happiness. A selfish child is discontented and restless. "The Lord will bless his people with peace" (Ps. 29:11).

How sweet it is to witness a child sharing his toys and presents with his playmates! You will find the sweetest response to these lessons of peacemaking in the heart of the little child. If he is old enough to quarrel, he is also wise enough to be taught to be a peacemaker. The earlier in life he learns to share with others, the easier it will be to become Christ-centered rather than self-centered. In mature years this same spirit of generosity will influence his actions and words. "But if ye bite and devour one another, take heed that ye be not consumed one of another" (Gal. 5:15).

After you have prayed about the problem of quarreling, and wisely dealt with it, do not think that no other misunderstandings will arise. You have not failed if another dispute occurs. Children are not perfect, and they must grow in Christian graces. When your child volunteers to be a peacemaker during a fracas, you can thank the Lord for this signal victory of the Holy Spirit in his heart. With such a triumph, your child has taken one forward step in the Christian warfare against self.

In teaching your child to be a peacemaker, use persuasion rather than force. Encourage your child to make his own choice. Be sure the balance falls in favor of the peacemaker. With prayer and wise direction you as a mother have the opportunity to mold early this tender, pliable nature. Keep it ever sensitive to the Lord's approval.

When parents are peacemakers between themselves, the child will readily recognize it and rejoice when Daddy and Mama do not quarrel. A home where peacemakers dwell is one of quietness. Quarreling keeps the house in confusion. Quarreling is an evidence of selfishness, greed, and unhappiness. Peace is the absence of strife. "Hatred stirreth up strifes: but love covereth all sins" (Prov. 10:12).

Others will recognize the beauty of Christian peacemakers. They will exclaim, "Truly, they are the children of God." Again, "For they shall be called [by observers] the children of God" (Matt. 5:9b).

The love of peace must originate in the heart.

When we see the fruit of peace budding in a little life, we know that there is a child of God. An attitude of love and consideration for others floods the hearts and lives of little peacemakers in a Christian home. Christ is our peace. This is "the gospel of peace." "Let us therefore follow after the things which make for peace" (Rom. 14:19).

The Ideal Mother

The heart of her husband doth safely trust in her.
—Proverbs 31:11

SAMUEL HAD A NOBLE mother who is a good example for us to follow. He had a noble father also. It is surprising to discover that all the wonderful mothers were equally wonderful wives. If we are going to be the kind of mothers God wants us to be, we must be loving and faithful wives.

Hannah was a loving wife, and her husband Elkanah loved and honored her. Hannah went regularly with him to the house of the Lord. Together they brought the sacrifices to God. Hannah prayerfully wondered why God had withheld the privilege of motherhood from her. She believed that children were a gift from God. Because she was childless, she wept with disappointment. She grieved and would not eat. Her sorrow of heart and lack of appetite troubled her husband because he loved her. He tried to cheer her up by asking, "Am not I better to thee than ten sons?"

Hannah sought the Lord with her problem. Burning tears accompanied the pouring out of her soul unto the Lord. Very likely she realized the need of a strong spiritual leader in Israel. "The Word of the Lord was precious in those days. There was no open vision." She realized the need of revival among her people. She knew of the corrupt lives of Eli's sons Hophni and Phinehas. She wanted a son who would be holy in his life and dedicated to God in his service. Year after year God postponed the answer to her prayer.

Hannah was unselfish. She promised to give her best to the Lord. She wanted her most precious possession to be used to God's glory. "I will give him unto the Lord all the days of his life," she vowed.

Hannah was a praying mother. During the feast at Shiloh she pleaded tearfully with the Lord to give her a son. When Eli knew that she prayed earnestly, he said, "Go in peace, and the God of Israel grant thee thy petition which thou hast asked of him." With this assurance from God's messenger, Hannah's "countenance was no more sad."

Hannah's faith was rewarded. God gave her the desire of her heart. Soon afterward she held in her arms a beautiful baby boy. He was to grow up to be a great leader for her needy people Israel.

Hannah remembered continually God's gracious

answer to her fervent prayers. She named her son Samuel which means "asked of God," or "name of God." Every time she called her son by name she was reminded again that God had heard her prayer and remembered her.

Hannah devoted her time to her baby while he was very young. She could have left her child with servants, but she preferred to devote herself to him. She was willing to forego the pleasure of a trip to Shiloh with her husband. When the time came for this annual journey, Hannah said to her husband, "I will not go up until the child be weaned, and then I will bring him, that he may appear before the Lord and there abide forever" (I Sam. 1:22).

Elkanah believed that Hannah had made a very wise decision. He respected her conviction that her duty was at home. A babysitter could not take Hannah's place. Elkanah replied, "Do what seemeth thee good; tarry until thou have weaned him; only the Lord establish his word" (I Sam. 1:23). Elkanah thought it would be hard for Hannah to give up Samuel as she had purposed. The husband was as conscientious as his wife in his determination to fulfill a promise to the Lord.

Hannah kept her vow to the Lord. When little Samuel was still quite young, she and Elkanah took him to live in the temple. This was to be his home all the days of his life. She told the prophet Eli that this little boy was the answer to her prayer. She had brought him to live with Eli so that he could be in full-time service in the house of the Lord. God granted Samuel many years as a prophet in Israel.

Hannah was rewarded many fold because of her sacrifice. God opened the windows of Heaven and poured her out great blessings. He gave her three sons and two daughters. "He maketh the barren woman to keep house, and to be the joyful mother of children" (Ps. 113:9).

Elkanah and Hannah continued their yearly journey to Shiloh to the house of the Lord. They came to worship God and also to visit little Samuel. Hannah made her growing boy a new and larger coat each year. Perhaps she wove it from the wool of their own flocks.

Samuel was left with the priest Eli to minister unto the Lord in the tabernacle. Hannah trusted that he would be divinely protected from the corruption and wickedness that prevailed. "And the child Samuel grew before the Lord."

Hannah's prayers were answered and fulfilled daily in the life of Samuel as he grew to manhood. He became a prophet of powerful influence. His preaching was effective. "The Lord was with him and did let none of his words fall to the ground" (I Sam. 3:19). God used him to judge Israel for forty years. The entire nation knew that "Samuel was established to be a prophet of the Lord."

Hannah is a classic example of a godly, consecrated mother. She raised her son for the Lord. God used

Samuel in a mighty way to bring the people of Israel back to God. He was a bulwark and a power to the nation. He was a counselor and an adviser to the king. His faithful life and ministry are still an inspiration to men today. May God give us many Hannahs and many Samuels to meet our nation's need!

Our Confidence

Cast not away therefore your confidence, which hath great recompense of reward.—Hebrews 10:35

IN THIS WORLD of uncertainty is there anything that we can be sure of? When everything changes so rapidly, is there anything that remains constant? Upon what can we base our confidence? "The Lord shall be thy confidence" (Prov. 3:26). "It is better to trust in the Lord than to put confidence in princes" (Ps. 118:9). Is our confidence in the Lord unfaltering so that we will trust Him anywhere? Can we say with Job, "Though he slay me, yet will I trust him" (13:15)?

"In the fear of the Lord is strong confidence: and his children shall have a place of refuge" (Prov. 14:26). Read the above verse over again. Memorize it and thus make it a bulwark for your soul. We are promised not only confidence, but *strong* confidence. This is a special provision for God's children. He has provided a place of refuge for them. Christ is that Refuge.

When persons frantically seek a place of safety, we know they feel themselves in great danger. It might be a storm or some other calamity from which they are fleeing. We are so frail of ourselves. But, "he knoweth our frame; he remembereth that we are dust. . . God is our refuge and strength . . . until these calamities be overpast. . . For thou hast been a strength to the poor, a strength to the needy in his distress, a refuge from the storm, a shadow from the heat, when the blast of the terrible ones is as a storm against the wall" (Ps. 103:14; 46:1; 57:1; Isa. 25:4).

No one escapes the storms of temptation and trial. Everyone is invited to flee to the place of refuge. There is no safer place than to be "in Christ." "The eternal God is thy refuge and underneath are the everlasting arms" (Deut. 33:27).

Do not despair in your distress and extremity. Put your confidence in Christ and in His comforting promises. "The Lord is good, a stronghold in the day of trouble; and he knoweth them that trust in him" (Nahum 1:7).

We relax in the everlasting arms and look up to exclaim, "Thy comforts delight my soul" (Ps. 94:19).

The word "confidence" can be thus illustrated: a child who has lost his way in the darkness stops crying at once when he finds his mother. If mother holds his hand, he feels that his safety is assured. Such should be our attitude of trust in our Lord Jesus Christ. He has promised, "For I the Lord thy God will hold thy right

hand, saying unto thee, Fear not; I will help thee"
(Isa. 41:13).

Just as we lean upon God for His care and guidance, so our little children rely upon us. From birth
they are utterly dependent upon their mothers for
food and protection. Mother guards their fragile spine
in babyhood. Soon they are able to hold up their heads
without support. When they take the first steps,
Mother's open arms give them the confidence that
they need. Their trust in her increases as their con-
sciousness unfolds.

Treasure your child's growing confidence through
the years. Preserve it by always telling him the truth.
Don't make impulsive promises that you will be unable to fulfill. A child does not easily forget these
youthful frustrations and disappointments. Shattered
expectations will weaken his faith in you.

Guard his confidence as a most precious possession.
Encourage him to tell you his secrets, his inward
thoughts, and his ambitions. Be a ready listener! Give
him an opportunity to confide in you. These confi-
dences are sacred. This kind of companionship with
your child will be one of your greatest joys. It compen-
sates for all a mother's daily labor and toil. It is worth
all the sleepless nights that you have spent in loving,
unselfish service.

Read Psalm 46, the Psalm of confidence and trust,
to your children at family worship time. As they listen,
it will enrich their lives and encourage them to trust

the Lord. It will nurture and deepen their faith. "Have no confidence in the flesh" but "trust in the Lord with all thine heart, and lean not unto thine own understanding" (Phil. 3:3; Prov. 3:5).

Discipline

If ye endure chastening, God dealeth with you as with sons.—Hebrews 12:7

GROWING BOYS AND GIRLS will be the men and women of tomorrow. You are training tomorrow's leaders. With such a goal in mind, mothers should realize the great importance of their task. This vision of the future should stimulate to extra effort in the training and discipline of children.

When we mothers begin to train a child, we are beginning the most important task in the world. Many mothers are poorly prepared, many employ the "trial-and-error" method in discipline. Our approach to each new problem is often crude and experimental. The best guideposts are found in the Bible. There we are given definite principles for the training of the young. Only the Christian mother who follows these principles can expect ultimate success. We are assured that if we "train up a child in the way that he should go, when he is old he will not depart from it" (Prov. 22:6). This is one of God's many directives. "Moreover by them is thy servant warned: and in keeping of them there is great reward" (Ps. 19:11).

42

During childhood, foundations of character are laid. Mothers must know something of building character if a little life is to develop spiritually strong. When the superstructure of a young life crumbles because of sin, it is usually because the foundation of his character had no real strength. It is a tragedy when the life of a teen-ager is wasted because of childhood neglect. "Correct thy son and he shall give thee rest; yea, he shall give delight unto thy soul" (Prov. 29:17).

Discipline must begin in early childhood. Each day will hold new adventures in discipline if one is alert. In the lives of most persons, early training determines the entire trend of adult life. Your child's moral and spiritual stamina will decide success or failure in mature years.

A number of psychologists and educators have been emphasizing unrestricted childish behavior and self-expression. They contend that in this way a child will develop his personality unhindered. But we are definitely warned against this procedure in the Bible. "A child left to himself bringeth his mother to shame" (Prov. 29:15).

At times there is need for the old-fashioned spanking and nothing else will do so well. "The rod and reproof give wisdom." Again: "Withhold not correction from the child, for if thou beatest him with the rod he shall not die. Thou shalt beat him with the rod and shalt deliver his soul from hell" (Prov. 23:13). Many modern parents shrink from this drastic method. The

43

Lord anticipated this reaction in a young mother's heart when He further advises: "Chasten thy son while there is hope, and let not thy soul spare for his crying" (Prov. 19:18).

Emotions of anger or pity should not influence the parent in the administration of punishment. Strict discipline will bring out the best traits in your child. He will be lovable and unspoiled. When he reaches school age, he will be a help to his teacher. Learning to read, write and spell will be a pleasure. The discipline of his mind will progress rapidly as a result of home training.

Every child is an individual problem. He must be dealt with prayerfully according to disposition and reactions. A mother needs divine wisdom to know how to encourage the best characteristics in each of her children. "If any of you lack wisdom, let him ask of God who giveth to all men liberally and upbraideth not; and it shall be given him" (James 1:5). Tactful discipline is truly the most difficult requirement of a mother's calling. It demands intelligence and perisistence. "For the Lord giveth wisdom: out of his mouth cometh knowledge and understanding" (Prov. 2:6).

Successful child-training is the result of extra effort and determination. There must be a constant expenditure of studied effort coupled with mother-love. "He that spareth the rod hateth his son: but he that loveth him chasteneth him betimes" (Prov. 13:24). If obedience is not learned at home it will be learned by bitter and humiliating experiences. "The way of trangressors is hard" (Prov. 13:15). You must be a good disciplinarian if you are to be a successful mother. "Foolishness is bound in the heart of a child, but the rod of correction will drive it far from him" (Prov. 22:15).

I once watched a young man take down storm windows and store them carefully in the basement for the summer months. He completed the job and returned the tools to the place where he secured them. He was cheerful, diligent and prompt. It was evident by his actions that his mother had trained him in neatness and precision. These traits had become habit. His Christian mother had been faithful and wise in training him. "Even a child is known by his doings, whether his work be pure and whether it be right" (Prov. 20:11).

How many times a parent has sadly regretted leniency in discipline! The results in the later life of their child have been heartbreaking. "A foolish son is a grief to his father and bitterness to her that bare him."

Foundations of Discipline

He openeth also their ear to discipline.—Job 36:10

IN THE PREVIOUS CHAPTER we considered building character and personality through discipline. This week we will consider the nature and substance of a strong foundation. The Christian faith is the only sure foundation for effective resistance against sin. In this world of wickedness an abundance of strength and bravery is needed to withstand the evil on every hand. The Lord Jesus Christ must be the cornerstone of a young person's life. Every other circumstance is dependent on this important decision. "For other foundation can no man lay than that is laid, which is Christ Jesus" (I Cor. 3:11).

Mothers, bring your children early to the Saviour. The mothers did this when Jesus was here on earth. "Then were brought unto him little children, that he should put his hands on them and pray" (Matt. 19:13). Luke tells us that the mothers brought unto Him also infants that He would touch them. Jesus urged the disciples to "Suffer the little children to come unto me and forbid them not, for of such is the kingdom of heaven" (Luke 18:16). Jesus loved the little children.

A two-months-old baby can understand one language—the language of love. Hold an infant in your arms and draw him a little closer to your heart. He will immediately feel that extra hug as a demonstration of tender love for him. He will look up into your face with a sweet appreciative smile. The language of love never needs words to express it. (Orphans suffer for lack of love.) The love of Jesus can become as real to a little child as his mother's love. "Whom having not seen, ye love."

When the spoken word is understood, the young

child will grasp quickly the wonder of his Saviour's love. He will understand by picture, song, and story that he is a precious lamb of the Good Shepherd's flock. He will say possessively, "The Lord is *my* shepherd." It is thrilling to a parent to witness the waking and unfolding of a child's intellect. His mind is like a delicate camera film. It is most sensitive to first impressions. A child's understanding is often clearer than that of a grown person whose mind is clouded by years of sin. "Out of the mouth of babes and sucklings thou hast perfected praise" (Matt. 21:16).

Perhaps some of you are thinking, "What has discipline to do with bringing our children to Jesus?" There is a very vital connection between the two. When Christ is received as Saviour, the Holy Spirit comes to dwell in the young person because he is now a child of God. A child in whom the Holy Spirit dwells will respond favorably to correction. The Lord's admonitions will elicit a ready response, and the Lord's own nurture is his also. These are the privileges of "sonship."

Now that the spiritual foundations are established, we will continue the subject of discipline. The mother who truly loves her child will curb his inclinations to evil. Just and loving training will inspire a loving response in a child's tender heart. His conscience is sensitive and is not "hardened by the deceitfulness of sin."

Do not slap your child in haste and temper. He deeply resents unfair treatment. It will rouse him to anger. "'Provoke not your children to anger lest they be discouraged" (Col. 3:21). The ability to remain calm while disciplining your children will be the result of patience and prayer.

Undisciplined children have been deprived of one of the greatest assets of character—self-control. Unrestrained appetites, uncontrolled tempers, unregulated habits of spending, carelessness in personal hygiene, stubborness, self-assertiveness, and disorderliness in the care of personal possessions are all disagreeable traits. They demand correction.

Perseverance is also taught by discipline. Half-done work at home and at school easily becomes a habit in childhood. A parent must insist on the finishing of a task once begun. Discipline is control and training, the restraining and curbing of an otherwise unmanageable will.

We all agree "that a wise son maketh a glad father, but a foolish son is the heaviness of his mother." We, therefore, should observe this scriptural advice, lest it be said of us, "But ye have set at nought all my counsel and would none of my reproof."

Mother, correct your child now while there is hope. "Therefore take fast hold of instruction; let her not go: keep her; for she is thy life" (Prov. 4:13).

More About Discipline

But I will teach you the good and the right way.
—I Samuel 12:23b

LIFE IS A DISCIPLINE. No one can escape discipline in school or in the world of business. A carefully planned routine at home will help your child adjust himself first in school life and later in his economic and social surroundings. Every service is a discipline. Marriage and its attendant responsibilities are a discipline. Our success or failure in our mature world is often determined by the way we have been trained to meet and overcome difficulties in the home.

Here is a phrase to hang up in the memory's gallery, "Forbearing threatening." Just two words, but exceedingly important in administering discipline. This phrase can be explained in two ways. First, never threaten a punishment which would endanger a child's safety or one that would be impossible to carry out. Sad words, when a mother shouts angrily, "I'll throw you in the garbage can!" Such ridiculous pronouncements will weaken your child's confidence in you. In some highly imaginative children it would create a terrible fear.

Second, when you declare a reasonable punishment, be sure to enforce it. Mothers often promise punishment which they never intend to carry out. The child repeats the same offense many times. The mother carelessly neglects the promised retribution. A wise, conscientious child often rebukes a parent for such forgetfulness, and reproves this terrible laxity. A slothful mother will overlook the repetition of a disobedient act. She herself lacks strength of character to enforce the disciplinary measure.

Forbear threatening, mothers! Be cautious and wise in declaring yourself. Then be sure you punish as you have promised. Discipline includes far more than corporal punishment. Other means of discipline are frequently more effective.

Happy is the child who has brothers and sisters who love him and compete with him. He certainly has the "edge" over an only child. He is constantly learning to adjust himself to the varying circumstances and distinct personalities that surround him. A family group is like the world in miniature. Dilemmas and problems will occur that present an individual challenge to every child in the home. There might be financial stringency; the entire household is keenly aware of it. Each one must brave the shortage cheerfully and make the best of what the Lord provides.

Younger members of the family often need help and sympathy from the older ones. Thoughtfulness and consideration of others are first practiced in ministering to younger brothers and sisters. They have many opportunities to "be kindly affectioned one to another with brotherly love." Practical lessons in extending sympathy are learned better through practice than by precept.

To be loving and kind to young members of a family often requires postponement of one's own pleasure. An unselfish older brother interrupts his interesting game to help some little brother in distress. Sometimes a whole day of expected recreation will be given up at the last moment to relieve a critical situation at home. The disappointment of upset plans is forgotten in love and service for the needy brother or sister. When brothers and sisters make such sacrifices for each other, they are being disciplined for life's hardest lessons.

A mother with only one child has to teach him many extra lessons of unselfishness and co-operation. Special wisdom in disciplining is needed in a small family.

Again, some parents shield their children from exacting duties. This is not a kindness to the child. The period of childhood is a small fraction of one's entire life. Responsibility is hard to shoulder if one has not borne it in the formative years of his life. The Bible says, "It is good for a man that he bear the yoke in his youth." We are bringing our children up to fill a place in the adult world. Remember they will not always be dependent and childish. The apostle Paul expresses this truth tersely, "When I was a child I spake as a child, I understood as a child, I thought as a child; but when I became a man I put away childish things."

Read the Word of God every day to your children. As they listen and come to know the Saviour, their ambition will be to please Him by their behavior. The Holy Spirit in their hearts strengthens this desire. They want their lives to glorify their Saviour when they grow up. Their acts are prompted by an inward motive not by outward compulsion. They want to sow wisely and well during their youth. May the yield in your child's life be abundant fruit not just useless leaves. Your training and prayer life, Mother, usually are the determining factors in the outcome.

Patience with Joyfulness

Strengthened with all might, according to his glorious power, unto all patience and longsuffering with joyfulness.—Colossians 1:11

IS ANY MERRY? Let him sing psalms." Joyfulness is our theme now! "My soul shall be joyful in the Lord." Joy is promised to us many times in Scripture. Jesus said, "These things have I spoken unto you," "that my joy might remain in you, and that your joy might be full." Our salvation is truly the source of our joy. Read all about this in Isaiah 12: "Therefore, with joy shalt thou draw water out of the wells of salvation."

Christ has sent His Holy Spirit into the world to give us "the oil of joy for mourning, the garment of praise for the spirit of heaviness." "Whoso trusteth in the Lord, happy is he." When the love of Christ floods our heart, then comes the joy .

To know this true joy, we must be free from the guilt of sin, free from anxiety during our lifetime, and free from fear regarding eternity. All these freedoms are found in Christ. Joy originates in Christ. He came that we might have His own joy. This joy is also the source of our strength (Neh. 8:10). When our thoughts are controlled by the joy of the Lord, worry and care are crowded out.

Joy is a prescription for good health. "A merry heart doeth good like a medicine. . . ." "He that is of a merry heart hath a continual feast" (Prov. 17:22; 15:15).

The joy of your heart is always reflected in your face. We are told in Proverbs that "a merry heart maketh a cheerful countenance." The observations of the Scriptures are as true now as when they were written.

Strange as it may seem, the joy of a Christian is deepened and increased by testings and trials. Trials tend to make the worldly person bitter and rebellious against his lot in life. The Christian soldier is given added strength to endure added trials. He is "strengthened with all might according to his [Christ's] glorious power unto all patience and long-suffering with joyfulness." Can you count it all joy when you "fall into divers testings"?

Sometimes a spirit of bitter resignation grows out of trials. This is not according to God's program. His will is that we be "patient with joyfulness," rather than being patient with bitterness. It is often arduous to be patient under trying circumstances, but to be *joyfully patient* is indeed still harder. It is an attitude which is a fruit of the Holy Spirit. We are partakers of Christ's life. Our supply of spiritual life is in Christ. Surrender your life afresh to your Saviour and Lord daily so that you can say, "Nevertheless I live, yet not I, but Christ liveth in me." Only as Christ lives in us can we be "more than conquerors through him that loved us." Gloom and melancholy are characteristics unbecoming saints of God.

Much joyful patience is required of a mother. It should be one of her outstanding virtues. From the moment a new-born baby first cries, through progressive stages of childhood the mother must exercise patience. Not only must the mother be patient, but be patient *with joyfulness.*

Disturbing incidents occur in family life which many mothers consider difficult crises. A joyfully patient mother prays for added grace at such times. She will not be disturbed by the unsettling occurrence but consider it as just another unexpected episode in the events of the day. "Continual patience with joyfulness" is needed to make a happy home.

A mother must be joyful when she is awakened sharply at night. Although she is tired, she must arise to tend her ailing child. Extra tenderness toward the little one will help her keep cheerful. She puts a cool hand on the hot forehead and gives a few reassuring pats to the child as she tucks him in for the second time. He will drop off to sleep so sweetly, with the happy certainty that Mother still loves him.

Quiet having been restored, she looks into the night sky, shiny with stars. She thanks the Lord for the opportunity and strength to do this extra nursing. Childless women, unless caring for other children, are denied this cherished privilege.

Then comes the trial of sickness which stretches out into weeks of isolation. As one child is convalescing, another one shows the alarming symptoms of the same disease. All the care must be repeated. Can a mother still be patient with joyfulness?

Yes, your life can be a testimony to your family and your neighbors. Many will not be aware of your patience, for it will be hidden under the panoply of joy. Other mothers, who have been tested as you are, will be encouraged by the abundant patience that underlies your joyfulness. Joy in your heart lightens all your duties and heightens all your pleasures.

Our earthly conditions vary daily. Our joy should not depend on changing scenes. "I will joy in the God of my salvation." *He* never changes.

We mothers often go to bed at night so tired that only faint echoes of cheer are ringing in our hearts. Weariness has almost crushed the joyfulness. "For so he giveth his beloved sleep." "Weeping may endure for a night, but joy cometh in the morning." A new day soon dawns, bringing with it new gladness.

The final consummation of joy will be in Heaven when we are "present with the Lord." "In thy presence there is fullness of joy: at thy right hand there are pleasures for evermore" (Psalm 16:11). Christ promises to present His children "faultless before the presence of his glory with exceeding joy." Anticipate with joy this bright future.

Unruly Tempers

Wherefore, my beloved brethren, let every man be swift to hear, slow to speak, slow to wrath.—James 1:19

A MOTHER'S TEMPER IS tested daily. Petty trials aggravate her patience and provoke her to wrath. Does she meet these difficulties by controlling the angry word, or does she fly into a rage at each new provocation? Irritability always becomes harder to control with every outburst of temper. The day that is started with a petulant attitude may end with headache and tears. The trivial annoyances become increasingly exasperating when we begin the day with unreasonable anger.

At breakfast time, the hot cereal cools off while mother waits for tardy sleepers to make their appearance. Indignation mounts with each minute of delay. Shall she tell the family what she thinks of late-comers, or shall she be longsuffering and gently reprove them for their laxity? All members of the family are finally assembled around the breakfast table, and with bowed heads, divine blessing and thanks is given for the food.

During the hasty meal, one of the children accidentally spills her glass of milk. The white liquid spreads all over the clean tablecloth, then unexpectedly it drips down on big sister's freshly ironed gingham dress. This is enough to aggravate an ordinary mother. But a Christian mother's reaction should be different. She does well to remember this proverb: "Whoso keepeth his mouth and his tongue, keepeth his soul from troubles."

Some persons are much more easily aroused than others. "He that is slow to anger is of great understanding: but he that is hasty of spirit exalteth folly" (Prov. 14:29).

Discussions on controversial subjects often become heated and end in angry words. The mother can be the referee in these disputes. Her tact can bring about a peaceful outcome in such a predicament. Declare your convictions firmly, Mother, then let the matter rest. Your silence will be more eloquent than wordy disputation. Controversy engenders discord. "A soft answer turneth away wrath; but grievous words stir up anger" (Prov. 15:1). Cultivate a calm manner when speaking. Choose "soft" words rather than vindictive phrases. Be courteous in tone and voice.

Discussions of political and economic subjects are often controversial. Try to avoid being stubborn and contentious in your own opinions. "It is better to dwell in the wilderness, than with a contentious and angry woman" (Prov. 21:19). Ask the Lord to enable you to appreciate the other side of the question. You may be surprised to find how you modify your opinion when you see the issue more clearly.

"The beginning of strife is as when one letteth out water: therefore leave off contention, before it be meddled with" (Prov. 17:14). Say little when you are angry. Hasty words do untold harm and can never be recalled. Let the trivial causes of dissension, bickering, and quarreling be overlooked. "Behold how great a matter a little fire kindleth."

It seems that the control of one's temper is akin to gentleness. David, in talking to the Lord, exclaims, "Thy gentleness hath made me great." The Lord lovingly forgives our faults and deals gently with our shortcomings. He does not chasten us in anger. "It is of the Lord's mercies that we are not consumed, because his compassions fail not. They are new every morning" (Lam. 3:22, 23). Just as the Lord does not deal with us in wrath, so we should not be impatient and angry with our children.

A person's violent temper usually is revealed in his facial expression. "'He that hath no rule over his own spirit is like a city that is broken down and without walls" (Prov. 25:28). A woman must be able to control her tongue before she will have any success as a mother. A quick temper ruins the tranquillity of a home. Children are attracted and charmed by gentleness.

A pleasure ride in the family car can often be the setting for argument and disagreement. The hotly contended disputes are usually over the street directions, the desired destinations, the speed to be maintained and the nature and number of purchases to be made. The opinions on each subject are as many and varied as there are passengers in the car. Everyone talks at once and no one is heard. Such a ride ceases to be a pleasure. Joseph's counsel to his traveling brothers is good advice for us today: "See that ye fall not out by the way." His words in modern language would be: "Be sure not to quarrel as you travel together!"

Military men are lauded for their deeds of conquest and valor. "He that is slow to anger is better than the mighty, and he that ruleth his spirit than he that taketh a city." It is just about as hard to control our tempers as it is for a general to conquer a city. What an analogy! As a general is acclaimed for his victories over the enemy, so we are highly commended for holding our temper. It is often our greatest foe.

After a hard day, the family gathers for the evening meal. Nerves are strained and tempers ready to flare up. Serve the dinner to the family quietly. The rough winds of argument will soon blow over and be dispelled. "Better is a dry morsel, and quietness therewith, than a house full of sacrifices with strife" (Prov. 17:1).

We mothers are women of discretion and understanding if we "defer our anger" and are not "hasty in spirit." Often a sharp word from Mother begins the day wrong for everyone. If we talk angrily to our children they will answer back irritably. Start each day by exchanging a smile and a bright good morning and greeting. Your family know you best. They will be quick to recognize your Christ-controlled temper. "She openeth her mouth with wisdom; and in her tongue is the law of kindness" (Prov. 31:26).

A Boy's Lunch

Seek ye first the kingdom of God and his righteousness, and all these things shall be added unto you.
—Matthew 6:33

I HAVE OFTEN THOUGHT of the little boy who gave his lunch to Jesus. The Lord and His disciples were resting on this grass-covered mountainside, near the sea of Galilee. Below them sparkled the blue waters of the lake. They watched the fishing boats sailing here and there in the distance.

Crowds of people were standing on the seashore. Some were walking up the mountain and searching for Jesus. Five thousand men had gathered to see more miracles of healing and to hear again wonderful words of truth, "for he taught them as one having authority and not as the scribes" (Mark 1:22).

Jesus had cured many who were diseased. Thousands of countryfolk had witnessed the healing of blind, lame, and deaf. The evidence of restored health and renewed strength proved to them that Jesus was the Son of God. What man could ever perform such miracles! "The blind receive their sight, the lepers are cleansed, and the deaf hear, and the poor have the gospel preached unto them."

What a crowd of people had assembled! The Bible tells us that five thousand men had gathered there, besides women and children. After they reached the place where Jesus was talking, they stood listening to Him for hours. Everything He said was so interesting and so wonderful. "Never man spake like this man."

The little lad with his picnic lunch of five barley loaves and two small fishes was there too. He dearly loved to listen to the Lord Jesus. He liked to stand as near to Him as possible. Jesus loved little children. He had said so, and the little boy believed it.

Our Lord viewed the hungry multitudes before Him. He planned to feed them before they started homeward. Such a miraculous supply of food would give them additional evidence that He was "God manifest in the flesh." Jesus asked Philip where he could get enough bread to feed all the people. Philip was puzzled at such a question. Jesus was testing his faith, "for he himself knew what he would do." His inquiry about the purchase of food started a discussion among the disciples. What could they do? Philip said, "Two hundred penny worth of bread is not sufficient for them that every one of them may take a little." None of the disciples would have that much money with him. And where would they have bought that much bread if they had had the money? Another disciple, Andrew, observed, "There is a lad here which hath five barley loaves and two small fishes: but what are they among so many?" This seemed such a useless suggestion. This single lunch was the only food available. Probably the five loaves were the size of bakery buns, and the two fishes dried and small.

Jesus wanted the disciples to know that the source of the food He would provide for the multitude was heavenly and not earthly. No material source of supply could be found to meet this stupendous need.

As the sun was going down toward evening Jesus told the disciples to seat the men by hundreds and by fifties. Then He took the lunch that the lad had given to Him. He blessed it and gave it to His disciples. They in turn distributed it to the seated multitude. Everyone ate heartily. There were twelve basketsful left over. Wouldn't it have been thrilling to be there? What a picnic!

The little boy had played a tremendous part in this outdoor feast. There were four different ways in which he could have disposed of his lunch. First, he could have selfishly refused to give his loaves and fishes to Jesus. We would never have heard of him if he had eaten them all himself. Second, he could have thrown his lunch away. This would have been foolish and wasteful. Third, he could have divided his lunch with those around him. The food would not have gone very far; no one's hunger would have been satisfied. Fourth, the little boy had the opportunity to give his lunch to

Jesus. He gave all he had to Jesus, and He multiplied it by thousands and thousands.

Let's give our lives to Jesus our Saviour as that little lad gave his lunch so long ago. "I beseech you therefore, brethren, by the mercies of God, that ye present your bodies a living sacrifice, holy, acceptable unto God, which is your reasonable service" (Rom. 12:1). The Lord will accept your gift and multiply your usefulness amazingly. He knows best how to increase the influence of your life unto His glory.

Young children have their entire life stretching before them. They too can give this most precious possession to Christ. Mothers, have you read or known of young men, seventeen years of age in jail for crime? They have thrown their young lives away. What were those mothers doing while the boys were growing up? Just a few years ago they were innocent, helpless babies. Now they are scarred by sin because, perhaps, their mothers did not faithfully pray with them and teach them God's Word.

Kneel down each day with your children and talk to God. The greatest joy in the world, mothers, is to watch a child grow in grace and in the knowledge of the Lord and Saviour Jesus Christ. What a contrast there is between a boy who lives for God and one who lives for this world! "And these words, which I command you this day, shall be in thine heart: and thou shalt teach them diligently unto thy children, and thou shalt talk of them when thou sittest in thy house, and

63

when thou walkest by the way, and when thou risest up" (Deut. 6:6, 7).

The Lord's Day

Remember the sabbath day, to keep it holy.
—Exodus 20:8

ACCORDING TO THE SCRIPTURES, our Sunday is the commencement of a new week. God has ordained this day as a spiritual haven of rest preceding the six days of activity.

"In the end of the sabbath, as it began to dawn toward the first day of the week," we behold Mary Magdalene and the other Mary coming to visit the sepulcher where the Lord Jesus was buried. They did not find Him there. He had risen from the dead. From that day to this, the worshipers of many lands have gathered together on the first day of the week to remember the glorious resurrection of our Lord. Sunday is a continuous memorial day of the resurrection of Christ from the grave, and for this reason it is set apart as a special day of worship in Christian homes. God has also ordained Sunday as a day in which our tired bodies will be renewed in strength.

Try devoting Sunday to Christian services and rest. Many people make home-building an excuse to stay away from the house of the Lord. Use Saturday for this purpose, and rest from toil on Sunday. Many families have followed this rule and have enjoyed the blessings which God has promised. Here is a promise from the Scriptures concerning the day of rest: "If thou turn away thy foot from the sabbath, from doing thy pleasure on my holy day; and call the sabbath a delight, the holy of the Lord, honorable; and shalt honor him, not doing thine own ways, nor finding thine own pleasure, nor speaking thine own words: then shalt thou delight thyself in the Lord; and I will cause thee to ride upon the high places of the earth, and feed thee with the heritage of Jacob thy father; for the mouth of the Lord hath spoken it" (Isa. 58: 13,14). Step out by faith upon this promise and experience these blessings for yourself and your household. "To obey is better than sacrifice and to hearken than the fat of lambs. . . . Whatsoever he saith unto you *do*" (I Sam 15:22; John 2:5).

Let us look in on a Christian family who are enjoying the Lord's day together. "This is the day which the Lord hath made; we will be glad and rejoice in it" (Ps. 118:24). It is early morning. The birds are beginning to chirp. The children are stirring in their beds. Some of them never sleep after sunup. No matter how late they retire or how quiet the house is, they wake up with the birds. There is no late sleeping in such a household!

Mother is the first one up. Sunday is going to be a rest day for her too. She has planned the day so that she can accompany her husband and children to Sunday school and to the morning church service. The family look forward to these happy weekends together. It is the highlight of family life and a truly joyous day. It is the culmination of the busy week, and a refreshing start for the following six days of toil. God in His graciousness has set aside this one day for the renewing of our spiritual life and the rebuilding of our physical energy.

On this glad morning, little hands hastily turned their pillows over to find the surprise mother had hidden there the night before. It might be a bright red apple or a small package of raisins wrapped in gay paper. "Under pillows" were always fun.

Then came the scrambling out of bed to dress up in the Sunday clothes. Mother had them laid out carefully near the children's beds after they had fallen asleep the previous evening. It was Sunday morning and there was always a spirit of expectancy and celebration. Breakfast was an outstanding occasion on that morning too. Crisp brown waffles were the mother's special treat. They were made in an electric waffle iron at the table. These were served with stewed peaches and hot chocolate. Mother never forgot to drop a white marshmallow into each steaming cup, as an extra touch. This differed greatly from the weekday menu. Then after a leisurely, cheerful meal everyone helped clear the table. The dishes were whisked away in a few minutes. The kitchen would be ready for instant use when the hungry family returned from church at noontime.

Mother allowed nothing to interfere with her going to the house of the Lord. Every other household duty was secondary. She taught a class of boys in the Sunday school. She prepared her Bible lesson in the evening hours.

"Scamper upstairs quietly now and put on your Sunday best," called Mother. "Be sure to remember your Bibles. Here is a dime for each one of you to put in the offering," she added; "hold it carefully so it will not be lost. It is the Lord's money, you know." For Mother conscientiously kept a little box marked "Lord's Treasury." The church money always came out of that box.

Next came the journey to the church. It was trying for some of the children to walk sedately so they skipped along instead. Just as they reached the corner where the church building stood, in rolled the big yellow Sunday school bus. There were children looking out of every window. Some sat behind the wide windshield apparently trying to help the patient driver.

"I was glad when they said unto me, Let us go into the house of the Lord."

Happy Memories

This is the day which the Lord hath made. We will be glad and rejoice in it.—Psalm 118:24

EVERY CHILD IS ENTITLED to a heritage of happy memories, entirely independent of riches or poverty. The far-reaching influence of early impressions will be in proportion to the adult companionship unselfishly given children in their formative years. Stored-up recollections will enrich and help mold manhood and womanhood. Mother's unfailing chumminess, often remembered, will often guide and calm a mature individual when he is confronted by temptation or sudden heartache. Fellowship with her in early years will link a lad's lonely heart with his mother's often-remembered prayers, laughter, and tears. Childhood years are storage years. Later, loneliness and solitude frequently draw upon memory's never-to-be-forgotten happy incidents. How about that lad of yours who will soon be eligible for the draft?

Attendance at church should be one of these treasured memories. It pays to instill this habit in growing children while they are young. Go with them to Sunday school and stay with them during church, that you may together "worship the Lord in the beauty of holiness."

In previous chapters, we watched the Sunday program of a Christian family. There may be minor variations in plans, but no other activity ever should interfere with the weekly appointment in the house of the Lord.

Some of us can make use of memory, now as we visualize the family sitting quietly in the church service. One hears again the great Shepherd's plea: "Fear not, little flock." Security is the rightful possession of a trusting child. The Lord Jesus knows the little lambs in His dependent flock. Each can personally say: "The Lord is *my* Shepherd." Such comfort from the Scriptures makes life free from childhood fears.

The minister closes his Bible. He has ended the message of the morning. The customary exhortation: "Let us pray," concludes the heart-to-heart talk. A gentle rustle stirs through the congregation. The organist resumes her place at the keyboard. The listeners reach for their hymnbooks. Voices blend in singing the ageless melody: "God be with you till we meet again."

Childish faces glow with happiness and contentment as the family starts the journey homeward. Everyone walks briskly; healthy appetites are sharpened by the anticipation of the coming meal. The food will be ready, having been planned and prepared the day before—a feast, abundant but simple. The most delicious dishes are chosen, and always served with the least amount of effort.

Father puts his key in the door, the lock is turned and Mother enters first. The children rush inside, brush past Father in haste. The best clothes are doffed and hung carefully away in readiness for the next Sunday morning. Clean, crisp washables are on in a jiffy.

A Sunday dinner has again fulfilled the expectations and needs of the hungry family. Quiet settles down on the entire household. Every drowsy and sleepy head is pillowed somewhere. Yes, it is the Lord's day for worship and rest. Mother has found the time at last, and the necessary quiet, to sit down and enjoy her favorite bit of reading, or is it a letter she is to write?

The rest-time is over, the children awaken with renewed energy to await the decision of Father as to the next move. Will it be a visit to cousins, or a walk into the hill country, which if taken, will be more of a race than a walk at times? What delight to explore the rolling hills where tall silver eucalyptus trees grow in great stretches of the uncultivated land! What pleasure to tussle with a strong wind, to watch the boats bob around on the beautiful lake! The sun travels fast toward the western horizon, while children squeal with joy at finding clumps of wild flowers. Then the slower and quieter trip—HOME!

Every mother of a growing family has the privilege of planning family life so that various happy memories of early years may sweeten and bless adult lives ever after. It takes advance planning, true, but oh, so little!

The Forward Child

Even a child is known by his doings, whether his work be pure, and whether it be right.—Proverbs 20:11

SOMEONE HAS ASKED how to deal with a forward child. We can give only a few suggestions. Some children are presumptuous, unreserved, bold, saucy, impudent, and unrestrained. Modesty and bashfulness are foreign to such personalities. A forward child is disliked by playmates, and has few friends.

Usually a problem child's parents have been over-indulgent with him. Meaning to be kind, they have done almost irremediable harm to the youngster. The forward child magnifies his own importance. He unfortunately thinks that the world revolves around him. What an awakening he experiences when he leaves the shelter of home, and finds the world uninterested in him! He discovers nearly everyone is antagonistic and hostile to his willfulness. He must now regain a normal viewpoint of his relationship to others. In so doing he may react unfavorably, becoming, morose, full of self-pity. He is unloved in school and in society. He is supremely selfish and thoughtless of others.

It is a kindness to a child to direct and curb strong desires. Wise control with loving guidance in the home will be doubly appreciated by a child when as an adult he steps out into the battle of life. The home is the first training ground for instruction and controlled conduct.

A forward child appropriates what he wants. His

71

parents have allowed him his own way. They have not used prayerful thought to develop the best qualities in him. Let no one think that careful training is an easy process. It requires strength of will and definite purpose. But to neglect instruction will result in much severer penalties. A self-willed child is oblivious to the feelings and needs of others. He knows nothing of humility, chagrin, or embarrassment. He insists on having the first chance at games, the largest portion on his plate, or the biggest piece of cake or candy. If he does not get what he wants, he sulks and pouts. His parents have given him his own way to "keep peace." This indulgence is not love. At the moment it is plainly the line of least resistance.

The motives of a bold child are all out of focus. His whole perspective will be forcibly changed some day, and then it will frustrate him. His own willfulness renders him weak and incapable of combat as he enters the mature world. He lacks "grit" and stamina which youthful self-sacrifices foster.

An incorrigible, saucy child is happiest when he is the center of all eyes. Company is invited to the home, then Junior occupies the center of the stage. Intelligent conversation between the host and guests is impossible. He stirs up a continual hubbub. He does not want to sit down lest he remain unnoticed. When the dinner is served, the menu does not suit his taste. He demands something different. His mother must rise from the table to satisfy his jaded appetite, or there will be no further peace at the meal. As it is, the guests have already lost their zest for the delicious meal. Conversation lags. Enjoyment of fellowship is impossible because of the constant furors and whining from the problem member of the family. Many readers will agree that this is not an exaggerated picture, nor is it an amusing predicament. What is the remedy for such a desperate situation? The distraught mother asks, "What can I do?"

Steps will have to be retraced, and there is a long way to travel. Remember, however, nothing is impossible with the Lord. It must be said that these faults of the willful child are directly traceable to inefficiency somewhere. Parents are the ones who need the correction. They have caused or will cause their child suffering and heartache. He must bear the brunt of adjustment one day.

If the parents persevere in prayer, the Holy Spirit will remake a child's misshapen nature. "Being confident of this very thing, that he that hath begun a good work in you will perform it until the day of Jesus Christ." Daily reading from the Word of God will swing the pendulum of self-pleasing toward the goal of Christ-control.

Your child needs firm, loving care. Discard haphazard methods. *Insist on obedience*. Be consistent in your statements, and carry them through. Never let him wield his power of will over your commands. Each time he wins a dispute, his own will and way will be more strongly entrenched. Teach him to control his temper and not to let it control him. Encourage unselfishness and thoughtfulness. Tell him that he will have to eat what is set before him or else go without food until the next meal. Show him that everything worthwhile in life is won by fair competition. Willfulness is never an asset.

"They that are of a froward heart are abomination to the Lord: but such as are upright in their way are his delight" (Prov. 11:20).

Stealing

Providing for honest things, not only in the sight of the Lord, but also in the sight of men.
—II Corinthians 8:21

OST OF OUR KNOWLEDGE is acquired experimentally. The child begins this learning process the day he is born. He learns by experience what sensations are connected with the satisfaction of his hunger. He learns to use and focus his eyes. Soon he learns to use his hands, and then he discovers his feet. He lifts his head and turns it from side to side to distinguish sound and its direction.

Knowledge in the moral realm begins at about nine months. He learns that "No, no," means some kind of prohibition. He soon learns the meaning of a smile and of a frown. And so he grows from day to day.

God has given you a little life to shape for Him. This is your responsibility, and you should do your utmost to discharge it faithfully in person.

Our special topic is the sin of stealing. We hear God speak: "Ye shall not steal, neither deal falsely, neither lie one to another." He says again: "Fear the Lord and depart from evil."

The habit of stealing is a cumulative one. It begins with acts apparently insignificant and unimportant. Nip the sin of stealing at first evidence and you will probably have no problem later on. Family worship and the reading of the Word of God are your greatest bulwark against this wrong. The fear of the Lord will shield your child from this evil.

A visitor comes to the home. Baby toddles over and takes possession of the purse that has been left on a chair. He soon has it opened and the contents promptly scattered over the floor. The mother's carelessness in allowing this is inexcusable. When she saw her child first go for the purse, she should have taken action. Her own purse should be equally inviolate. All purses must be respected and left untouched. The baby can be taught to ignore a purse as a forbidden pleasure. He can learn to respect others' property so early in life so that it will seem to him later that he always knew. The older brothers and sisters may have toys and trinkets that a baby should be taught not to touch or to play with. He should have toys that belong to him exclusively. He will exhibit the joy of possession by saying, "Mine," every time he holds one of his own treasures.

Perhaps a child is fond of candy. His mother has said "No" when he wanted a piece. She explained that it would spoil his appetite. There the candy lay in a transparent glass dish within reach of the child's outstretched hand. The temptation is too great and the child snatches a piece. He shows guilt in his manner and betrays duplicity. The mother must be watchful and curb this disobedience. She can take the half-eaten candy out of his mouth and put the dish on a higher shelf. Now comes the tact and wisdom in this training.

The mother takes her child on her lap or sits beside him on the davenport. She has a confidential heart-to-heart talk about the sin of stealing. She aims to make the correction interesting, and she avoids being arbitrary and despotic. She captures the interest of the child and reasons with him, letting him see that the right way is always the best way. He soon will enjoy sharing mutual ideals of Christian conduct. Then she kneels down with him and talks to the Lord about the circumstance. The devil cannot win over a combination like that.

Family worship each morning will give additional opportunity for chats however brief they must be. This will be continuation of the precepts taught every day. They will register on his heart and deter him from stealing.

A wise mother tells her child that there is a time

and place for eating candy. He can have a piece after dinner. At this opportunity she can pass the dish to him with ceremony and the child will graciously take a piece with a smiling "Thank you." Then he may pass the dish to others present. He will love this and will learn that legitimate pleasures are the most fun. As a good boy, everyone will enjoy eating a piece with him after dinner.

Suppose the mother takes her small child to the store. Luscious fruits are displayed on the shelves. The child helps himself to a grape. Mother notices this and sternly forbids it. This is the negative side of the training, but she can also give a bit of the positive: she explains that those grapes are not theirs; they should not take them. The clerk is on duty to serve them. If they want grapes, they will buy them. Mother orders a small amount of grapes, and allows her child to pay for them. He can also have the fun of carrying his purchase home. He has learned another valuable lesson in a short time. He has learned to respect the owner of the produce. He has learned what money will do and how to use it. He has a lawful possession that he can enjoy and share with his brothers and sisters.

It is deplorable for a mother to allow her child to help himself to apples from the grocer's pile. He is stealing, and such an act cannot be regarded lightly. A child who steals and is not corrected grows bold and unmanageable. He will grow up to think nothing of stealing time belonging to others, among other things.

You will subject him to correction by outsiders if you do not curb him yourself. This will harden his conscience and breed rebellion and stealthiness in his actions.

Mothers, wake up! Don't be the cause of your child's sin and shame! The command is, "Thou shalt not steal." "Providing for honest things, not only in the sight of the Lord, but also in the sight of men" (II Cor. 8:21).

A New Year's Resolve

The Lord will give grace and glory.—Psalm 84:11a

WE ARE ENTERING a new year filled with new opportunities, new horizons, and new challenges. There will be new difficulties and new victories, too. We do not know what the coming year holds for any of us, but we do know that God foresees our future. The paths unseen by us are not unknown to Him.

There is a Bible verse in Psalm 45 that we mothers can choose for our goal. Keep this verse uppermost in your mind and thought. Make it a prayer request too. "The king's daughter is all glorious within."

How can we be the King's daughters? How can we be glorious within?

Christ is King of kings and Lord of lords. Therefore if we belong to Him, we are daughters of a King—

daughters by adoption. We are children of God by faith in the Lord Jesus Christ.

Glory means heavenly beauty. "There is one glory of the sun and another glory of the moon and another glory of the stars, for every star differeth from another star in glory." Your life can also be radiant with a heavenly glory by the Holy Spirit. "He dwelleth with you, and shall be in you."

Your life must be pure and clean if the glory of the Lord is to be seen in it. This means a daily cleansing from sin. We can only be glorious within if we are pure in heart. "Blessed are the pure in heart for they shall see God." How can we be cleansed from sin? "If we confess our sins, he is faithful and just to forgive us our sins and to cleanse us from all unrighteousness."

When there are glimpses of glory in your actions and words, remember it is not you but "Christ in you, the hope of glory." Apart from Christ you can never be glorious within. "Ye are our epistle . . . written not with ink, but with the Spirit of the living God; not on tables of stone, but in fleshly tables of the heart" (II Cor. 3:2, 3).

The Scriptures continue with this story of glory. When Moses finished writing the Ten Commandments on two tables of stone, his face shone with divine glory. We are told that when he came down from the mountain from this meeting with God, the people could not look at him because of the brightness of his countenance. If Moses' face glowed with the glory of

79

God because he spent forty days in His presence, should not the life of a Christian be beautiful? His heart is filled with this same Holy Spirit. "How shall not the ministration of the Spirit be rather glorious?" (II Cor. 3:8).

We feel hopeless when we consider our human frailties and weaknesses. Christ is our only hope of glory. It is Christ in you, the hope of glory.

Christ Jesus our Lord is truly glorious. "We all with open face beholding as in a glass the glory of the Lord, are changed into the same image from glory to glory even as by the Spirit of the Lord" (II Cor. 3:18). Only the Holy Spirit can give you heavenly beauty and make you glorious within. "For man looketh on the outward appearance, but God looketh on the heart" (I Samuel 16:7). Wouldn't you rather have a Christ-like character than have a veneer of physical beauty? The first is stable and lasting, the second is superficial and of secondary importance.

Oh, that each one of us might be glorious within! It is our hearts that must be glorious, for out of the heart are the issues of life. Let us not be of those "that glory in appearance and not in heart." Each time you read the word "glory" in family worship from now on, it should have a richer meaning.

The Holy Spirit transforms our hearts into Christ-likeness. He is our life. "Christ liveth in me; and the life that I now live in the flesh I live by the faith of the Son of God who loved me and gave himself for me"

(Gal. 2:20). When Christ is our life, our boast will not be in ourselves. "Therefore glorify God in your body and in your spirit which are God's."

A mother who belongs to Christ should display attributes of glory and heavenly beauty in her home. The following virtues are characteristics which accompany her salvation. "She openeth her mouth with wisdom and in her tongue is the law of kindness. . . . Strength and honor are her clothing, and she shall rejoice in time to come. . . . The heart of her husband doth safely trust in her. She will do him good and not evil all the days of her life. . . . Her children arise up and call her blessed, her husband also, and he praiseth her" (see Prov. 31). Explore the Scripture for additional rare and outstanding traits of Christian character.

"Lord Jesus, I am Thy daughter. Make me more like Thyself. Make me all glorious within. Amen."

Truthfulness

Remove from me the way of lying.—Psalm 119:29

THE MOST IMPORTANT PART of a mother's high calling is to bring her children up in the nurture and the admonition of the Lord. Each child must be taught lessons of behavior every day. The character of a child is built gradually. The Lord tells us to teach "precept upon precept, line upon line, here a little, there a little." Your children will learn the difference between right and wrong as they play and work with you. It is so important that a mother be the companion of her children. Child-training is your special job. You cannot hire it done and expect very good results. Ask the Lord to prosper your husband in his work so that you will not have to go out into the business world and leave your children in another's care.

The Bible tells us that we are to bring the children up in "the nurture and admonition of the Lord." Those two words "nurture and admonition" should be in your prayer each day. The Lord's nurture is His constant loving care of a little child. The Lord's admonitions are His gentle warnings and wise instruction found in the Bible. Very definite guidance is given to us on the pages of God's Holy Word. "All scripture is profitable for doctrine, for reproof, for correction, and for instruction in righteousness." We as mothers desire to teach our children these admonitions so that they will be steadfast Christians. Then we can say to each one of our children, as Paul said to young Timothy, "From a child thou hast known the holy scriptures, which are able to make thee wise unto salvation, through faith which is in Christ Jesus." The Holy Spirit is given to us to help in this nurture, because the task is too big for us to attempt in our own strength and wisdom.

Perhaps you discovered one day that your child

was not telling the truth. He always had an active imagination and often told fantastic stories. But now, to your sorrow, you discover he is forming the habit of lying. It is time to teach him to distinguish between truth and falsehood.

Together you can open God's Word and find out what He says about lying. You have taught your child in family worship to reverence and believe God's Word. God's opinion of lying is found in Proverbs 12:2: "Lying lips are an abomination unto the Lord: but they that deal truly are his delight." Explain that the word "abomination" means something abhorrent (something to shrink from). The boy who tells the truth, however, is a delight to His Saviour and certainly to his mother. Your child is not too young to comprehend this truth. It is often a source of wonder how quickly a child can understand the Bible. The Lord Jesus thanked the Father one day that He "had hidden these things fom the wise and prudent and had revealed them unto babes."

Repeat this verse over and over to your growing child: "Lying lips are an abomination to the Lord: but they that deal truly are his delight." It will soon be memorized by frequent repetition. It will ever remain in his mind as a pattern for action. As you explain God's attitude toward lying, as revealed in this verse, your child will understand that God is grieved by falsehood, but delighted with him when he tells the truth.

The first time your child tells a lie, let him know that he is not deceiving you. Often the Lord gives a mother special perception in this regard. Every time your child tells the truth, be sure to recognize it and commend him for it. Here is an illustration.

You have very special China dishes. They are a few of the presents you received at your wedding. You have guarded them through the years. The family know how much you treasure your beautiful flowered plates. One day your little boy broke one accidentally—the little boy that you have patiently been teaching to tell the truth. You discovered your plate broken beyond mending when you returned to the room. At first you were grieved and indignant. You inquired who had been so careless. Your little son said hesitantly, "I did it, Mommie." He looked frightened as he confessed it, for he feared punishment, but he had dared to tell the truth.

In a case like that, forget your own loss and clasp him in your arms. Tell him he has made you so happy *because he told the truth*. The Lord Jesus is pleased with the child too because "they that deal truly are his delight."

Together you sweep up the broken pieces on the dustpan and throw them away. You admit that you are sorry the plate is gone, and you tell him why. You suggest that he be careful in the future. There will be no question that when your son reaches manhood he will cherish this incident as one of his choice memories. He will never forget the punishment he escaped or the sorrow he felt for his carelessness. He experienced also a great satisfaction in telling the truth. He discovered that he and his mother were chums. He would feel free from now on to tell all his troubles to her because she understood.

In some such way the bonds of your love for each other become strengthened day by day. Nothing can take the place of companionship. Nothing can give you more joy. This happiness is yours as you bring your children up in the nurture and admonition of the Lord.

Here are additional nuggets of truth found in God's Word concerning truthfulness: "I have chosen the way of truth" (Ps. 119:30). "A righteous man hateth lying. . . . A faithful witness will not lie" (Prov. 13:5; 14:5). "He that speaketh lies shall not go unpunished" (Prov. 19:5). "Lie not one to the other" (Col. 3:9). Revelation 21:8 includes "all liars" in its account of final awful judgment.

Athletics — Wrestling

And every man that striveth for the mastery is temperate in all things.—I Corinthians 9:25

THIS MESSAGE IS ESPECIALLY written to mothers of sports-minded boys. Mothers should have a fairly intelligent idea of football, baseball, basketball, track, and wrestling. Knowing the meaning of terms used in each game will help you understand your boy's conversation. He usually comes in shortly before supper, his hair a little tousled. He is glad to sink into an easy chair and relax for a minute. He smells the food cooking and he can figure out almost the whole menu. Then he starts to tell you about his victories and losses. Untie your apron and take it off; sit down on one of the dining room chairs and give the boy your undivided attention. If you want to be an appreciative and understanding mother, you will have to be on your toes to grasp everything about the afternoon practice. Here and there you will have to give some comment so that the conversation will not be one-sided. Your son wants a ready listener. A teen-age boy loves to unburden his heart to someone. Who could be better than his own "mom"?

One day I was wondering what sanction there could be for wrestling. Jacob was a contestant in the first recorded wrestling match. Wrestling requires skill and prowess. This wrestling of Jacob and the man of God has intrigued innumerable readers down through the ages.

Jacob had crossed the ford Jabbok. He had left his family and possessions on the other side of the brook, "and Jacob was left alone" (Genesis 32:24). (Solitude is often the best time to talk things over with your Saviour. Steal away from everyone, spread the Bible out before you and find God's viewpoint on your problem. Then talk to Him about it.)

Jacob recalled the promise that God had made to him after he had fled from his brother Esau long ago. The first lonely night away from home he had spent under the stars. He used a stone for his pillow as he slept. God had visited him during the nightwatches and had spoken these comforting words: "And behold I am with thee and will keep thee in all places whither thou goest." Jacob believed God's promise to him and treasured it in his heart during the years. Twenty years had passed. Jacob was returning to the land from which he had fled. He prayed that God would fulfill His promise to him in this hour of great need.

Jacob was face to face with a reconciliation that had been postponed for twenty years. He had cheated his brother Esau out of his birthright when they were young men. In the morning, this lifelong feud would have to be settled. He realized his need of courage. He confessed the fraud that had caused his exile.

When Jacob acknowledged his past sins and short-comings, God forgave him. "I am not worthy of the least of thy mercies, and of all the truth thou hast showed thy servant." Does this prayer express the utter unworthiness you feel in your own life? It left Jacob prostrate at the throne of mercy. The situation could be saved only by God's intervention.

Jacob had character and purpose. He had lived a rugged outdoor life. He had battled the cold, the drought, and heat of summer. He had been ever on the alert to defend his flocks against the wild beasts that stalked them. Seven times he had safeguarded his business interests from the greed of his partner, Laban. Now a greater crisis loomed, an inescapable one. Read the whole story of this great wrestling match in Genesis 32:24-32.

"And there wrestled a man with him." This was a physical combat, as well as a spiritual struggle. Jacob's hip was thrown out of joint during the fray, and he limped the rest of his life. The contest continued throughout the night. Jacob held on tenaciously. He had not "pinned" his problem yet. He had not won the match. He was holding his own, but he wasn't a winner. Victory is costly, but defeat is far more costly.

Jacob's opponent pleaded, "Let me go, for the day breaketh." It was morning, but Jacob wrestled on. He was panting, and nearly exhausted. In pain and desperation he cried, "I will not let thee go except thou bless me." Wrestling challenges all that is in a man and then calls for that extra effort that stretches beyond ordinary endurance. Jacob was desperately in earnest.

Yes, he had faith as he wrestled on with tenacity and persistence! Worn out with the struggle but still importunate, he held on saying, "I will not let thee go except thou bless me." Jacob was out for God's blessing. He would not be satisfied with anything less. The Lord honored his faith and rewarded it with this commendation: "As a prince hast thou power with God and with man, and hast prevailed." Strength to win when defeat seems imminent—that is power. "And he blessed him there." It is interesting to realize that it was God who met Jacob face to face.

"And as he passed over Peniel, the sun rose upon him, and he halted upon his thigh." Jacob bore the marks of that wrestling as long as he lived. This infirmity was a constant reminder of the price he had paid for God's everlasting blessing. It was gloriously worth the agonizing struggle and the price.

No one has come out victoriously on the Lord's side who escaped the hand-to-hand conflict to obtain the victories of faith. The visible rewards of faith are granted only to those who, like Jacob, have met God face to face and have prevailed. Every conflict can become a stepping stone to greater victory. "Thanks be unto God who always causeth us to triumph in Christ" (II Cor. 2:14).

Perhaps it would be good to encourage your boy to wrestle. It is a healthy sport. It will develop in him initiative and dogged determination. He needs these qualities as he prepares to make his living in the world. Best of all, it will teach him some great lessons in the warfare that will come, when he meets opposition in living a clean, Christian life.

Forgiveness

For thou, Lord, art good, and ready to forgive.
—Psalm 86:5a

I T IS CHRISTLIKE TO forgive, and it is our Saviour's plan that we be like Him. He is full of grace and truth. He came to earth to give His life for sinners so that He could forgive us; and He shows us how to forgive others.

The Lord Jesus lived a life of forgiveness all through His earthly ministry. His love for us brought Him down from the glories of Heaven to the sorrows of earth. Although He poured out His life in healing the sick and strengthening the weak, "he was despised and we [they] esteemed him not." He went about doing good, and was hated and reviled. He became "obedient unto death, even the death of the cross" for our sins. He forgave us all when we were unlovely. We are told to forgive one another, "even as God for Christ's sake hath forgiven us."

We can start the habit of forgiveness in the family circle. Bitterness can take root, it can spring up and choke the springs of happiness. An unforgiving spirit darkens the atmosphere of a home. It casts a shadow on dispositions. It creates a spirit of unrest and discord.

Family worship is the time to clear up misunderstandings in the home. Ask God to teach everyone the joy of forgiveness daily. It is a spiritual triumph to forgive. "Let not the sun go down upon your wrath." The bitterness of an unforgiving spirit is like a noxious weed. If it becomes rooted in the human heart, it is hard to eradicate.

Forgive your husband, forgive your children, forgive your neighbors. Forgive those who work with you in Sunday school and church. Don't harbor a grudge against anyone. This leads to the unchristian desire to return evil for evil. Each one has his peculiar frailties and weaknesses. Overlook these and love your fellow Christians. "Love suffereth long and is kind." If we recompense evil for evil, the Holy Spirit will be grieved, and our growth in grace will be halted. Our aim in life is to be healthy, Spirit-filled, growing Christians. We must ever press onward and upward in the service of the Lord. Unforgiveness in our hearts makes us bitter; forgiveness will flood our souls with joy.

Forgiveness in the heart will be evident in speech and actions. Your children will unconsciously pattern their lives after yours. They will be bitter toward their little friends if they know you are bitter toward yours. Your children will forgive when they notice you forgive.

You will forget wherein you were wronged, if you forgive. God has forgiven our iniquities and remembers them no more. If God forgets so should we. We cannot forgive in our own strength, especially if the hurt is deep. It takes grace to forgive. The Lord Jesus, through the Spirit, imparts this grace. In after years when your children make a decision to forgive, they will remember how Mother always forgave, and they will emulate her. Be an outstanding example of forgiveness to your children.

Sometimes we ask impatiently, "Do I have to keep on forgiving and forgiving endlessly?" Peter asked the same question. "How often shall my brother sin against me and I forgive him? till seven times?" Jesus saith unto him, "I say not unto thee, Until seven times: but, Until seventy times seven." Multiply this for yourself. You will see that we could not possibly count these incidents of forgiveness. They will soon go unnumbered.

It is Christike to forgive when you have real cause for wrath. This is your opportunity to gain the victory over the quick, ungracious word and the cruel answer. "But if, when ye do well, and suffer for it, ye take it patiently, this is acceptable with God" (I Peter 2:20). If we are misquoted, slighted and overlooked, if even our motives are misunderstood, let's forgive. "Even as Christ forgave you, so also do ye."

We hear the Lord Jesus praying for those who nailed Him to the cross. "Father, forgive them, for they know not what they do." We marvel at such forgiveness. We worship with bowed hearts in deep reverence. This glorious sacrifice and majestic forgiveness wrought our great salvation, "which . . . the angels desire to look into."

When Jesus was born, Heaven couldn't contain the angelic praise of His advent. The multitudes of the heavenly hosts burst into song, "Glory to God in the highest and on earth peace, good will to men." Peace and good will are ever the fruits of divine forgiveness;

peace toward God and good will toward those we know.

Oh, that we might become more like our forgiving Saviour! God has called us that we might "be conformed to the image of his son." "But we all, with open face beholding as in a glass the glory of the Lord are changed into the same image from glory to glory, even as by the Spirit of the Lord.'

Thanksgiving and Thanks-living

In everything give thanks: for this is the will of God in Christ Jesus concerning you.—I Thessalonians 5:18

IF WE WROTE DOWN all the blessings that God showers upon us daily, the list would be a long one. Not the least of these divine favors would include the many automobile excursions we have made without mishap. These trips have covered thousands of miles. Figure out for yourself the great distances that were traveled by members of *your* household. While driving along the highways, not one accident occurred. There were no mechanical failures to mar the pleasure trips. Not even a tire needed changing. Have we thanked God for protecting us? Sometimes an inch or two has meant the difference between life and death. The Lord in His mercy granted us that inch, and life.

"Thou crownest the year with thy goodness" (Ps. 65:11). The Lord has truly crowned our lives with His goodness. His showers of grace, bounty, and blessing have been poured down upon us. "O Lord how manifold are thy works! the earth is full of thy riches" (Ps. 104:24). Most of these blessings we accept without thanking the Giver of them.

Food for our sustenance was grown on acres and acres of farmland. Refreshing rain has fallen on the fertile fields. Our sources of milk, meat, and flour depend upon this rain from heaven "which watereth the earth." "Thou, O God, didst send a plentiful rain." It would be impossible to plow the thirsty earth and sow it with seed unless it was watered from above. "Thou makest it soft with showers, thou blessest the springing thereof." Let your children know these things when you bow your head at mealtime to give thanks to the Lord. His provision is so abundant. "Bless the Lord, O my soul, and forget not all his benefits" (Ps. 103:2).

When friends do us a kindness, it is often our practice to return that kindness in some way. Do we feel obligated to the Giver of every good and perfect gift in the same way? Is our sense of appreciation keen and alert? "What can I render unto the Lord for all his benefits toward me?" How can we show our thanksgiving for divine blessing? "Oh, that men would praise the Lord for his goodness, and for his wonderful works to the children of men" (Ps. 107:8).

A thankful spirit is a normal Christian attitude. It is a spontaneous response to all of God's goodness. A song springs to our lips when our hearts are overflowing with thanksgiving. "I will sing unto the Lord as long as I live: I will sing praise to my God while I have my being. My meditation of him shall be sweet" (Ps. 104:33, 34) . Singing hymns at housework will lighten any task. Let our song be an anthem of praise, a paean of thanksgiving. "For the Lord is great and greatly to be praised; . . . sing unto the Lord with the voice of thanksgiving."

"Blessed be the Lord who daily loadeth us with benefits, even the God of our salvation." The men and women on the farflung mission fields have shown their appreciation for these benefits by giving their lives in service. The heathen have been made glad by the message of salvation. They have been loosed from their terrible bonds of sin and fear. They have come out into the liberty wherewith Christ hath made them free. All this, because abounding gratitude to God propelled these missionaries into foreign lands, to share this great thanksgiving with others. They could say: "The love of Christ constraineth us."

What can we mothers render unto the Lord for all His benefits? We may not be able to go across the seas as missionaries, but we can make it possible for others to go. Certainly we should be willing to send our sons and daughters in our stead. We can acquaint our children daily with a knowledge of God's bounty and blessing by reading the accounts of His kindness in the Word of God.

God has given these children to us to rear for Him.

When they grow up, they will either be the servants of self and sin or joyful servants of their Saviour Jesus Christ. They cannot serve two masters. This is the time to foster heartfelt gratitude to the Lord. Teach them to be thankful. Tell them what great things the Lord has done for them.

"In everything give thanks, for this is the will of God in Christ Jesus concerning you." Does "everything" include your trials too? Can you thank the Lord for the hard experiences you have weathered? Our difficulties reveal our frailties and compel us to be utterly dependent upon the Lord who is our strength.

We are dismayed by the pilgrimage through the valley of dark clouds and gloomy shadows. But where there is a valley there are always hills. At their crest the sun always feels warmer and shines brighter. Let us go on to the hilltop of victory! "Though I walk in the midst of trouble, thou wilt revive me." And again, "Thou hidest thy face, and they are troubled." But faith is always victorious: "Yea though I walk through the valley of the shadow of death, I will fear no evil, for *thou art with me.*" David gave his victorious testimony: "I called unto the Lord in my distress, and the Lord answered me, and set me in a large place."

Let us express our thanksgiving with our lives as well as with our lips. We are crowding our storehouses full of good things. Let us be sure the supplies for God's house and His work do not decrease. "Bring ye all the tithes into the storehouse, and prove me now herewith, saith the Lord, if I will pour you out a blessing that ye will not be able to receive." Let us share our prosperity with the Lord. "Not grudgingly, nor of necessity; for God loveth a cheerful giver." It pays to give generously to the Lord. It may mean a sacrifice on your part, but that is the kind of giving that is really worth while. "And let them sacrifice the sacrifices of thanksgiving and declare his works with rejoicing."

We mothers have been on the receiving end for so long that we should start giving for a change. Especially the giving of thanks. Let our "hearts be filled with thanks and our hands filled with giving." We all can give thanks at mealtime. Around the dining table, in the morning, at noon, and again at eventide, let us fold our hands, bow our heads, and thank the Lord for our food.

Heart Trouble

Be of good courage, and he shall strengthen thine heart.—Psalm 27:14

WE ARE TOLD THAT heart disease leads the list of fatal illnesses today. We are urged to co-operate in the campaign against this prevalent malady. There may have been a high death rate from heart trouble in Bible times, too. A great deal is said about the functions of the heart in Scripture. We are persuaded that the holy Word of God is a very up-to-date book. It maintains its place as the "world's best seller."

The divine cure for heart trouble always accompanies the described weaknesses. Our physical well-being is definitely linked with our spiritual health; one reacts upon the other. In III John we read, "Beloved, I wish above all things that thou mayest prosper and be in health, even as thy soul prospereth."

The type of heart trouble I am thinking about now can actually be transmitted. Our lives are closely bound up with one another. "For none of us liveth unto himself, and no man dieth unto himself." Courage always begets courage. Defeatism is likewise contagious. Fear is communicable. When an ancient army was mobilized, certain rules were declared. Cowards did not make good soldiers. The assembled recruits were asked: "What man is there that is fearful and fainthearted? Let him go and return unto his house, lest his brethren's heart faint as well as his heart." Let us be stouthearted and say, "God is the strength of my heart and my portion forever." The Book of Proverbs says, "A sound heart is the life of the flesh." We are physically strong only as our heart is strong. Emotions play a major part in the maintenance of a healthy heart. High tension joy needs our attention as well as over-much grief.

Perhaps the family has been praying at worship for a different place of work for Daddy, or for needed clothes, or perhaps a substantial raise, or maybe for a new home in another district. It seems as if prayer has not been heard. But God is faithful and "His ear is open to the righteous." Then suddenly everything happens at once. What a thrill! "Hope deferred maketh the heart sick: but when the desire cometh, it is a tree of life."

The heart noticeably increases its tempo and the force of its pulsation when one is alarmed by bad news or startled by sudden catastrophe. David cried out: "My heart panteth, my heart faileth me." Today's senators and congressmen in these United States voice their concern for our future. The Lord Jesus foretold this bewilderment. He said that we would behold "men's hearts failing them for fear, and for looking for those things which are coming on the earth; for the powers of heaven shall be shaken."

Israel was told by his eleven sons that his long-lost Joseph was alive and ruling Egypt. "Jacob's heart fainted, for he believed them not." He came to the tent door to see the wagons that Joseph sent to carry him to Egypt. He accepted this concrete proof that his son was truly alive, and "the spirit of Jacob their father revived."

Eli died suddenly when he heard that the ark of the Lord had been captured. The enemy had penetrated into the inner sanctuary of his nation's most sacred possession. The shock of this defeat caused the death of the elderly priest. "For his heart trembled for the ark of the Lord."

Nabal was a rich man, but selfish and stingy. Though he had more wealth than he could use himself, he refused to share it with others. Abigail, his wife, was gracious and generous. She gladly paid a debt of gratitude to the men who deserved it. Nabal caroused with his friends and knew not of his wife's generosity. "It came to pass in the morning, when the wine had gone out of Nabal, and his wife had told him all these things, that his heart died within him and he became as a stone." Nabal evidently suffered a stroke. His intemperance and unjustified anger gave him high blood pressure. The attack proved fatal. "Talk no more so exceeding proudly; let not arrogancy come out of your mouth: for the Lord is a God of knowledge, and by him actions are weighed."

David, the "sweet singer of Israel," was often deeply stirred. He put into words the feeling you and I cannot adequately express. "My flesh and my heart faileth, but God is my portion forever." David also suffered greatly. His sorrows and disappointments taught him to flee to God as his refuge and protector. "The troubles of my heart are enlarged; O bring me out of my distresses" (Ps. 25:17).

Nehemiah heard that Jerusalem was falling in ruins. He loved his homeland and mourned over its reported decay and destruction. Nehemiah wept, mourned, fasted, and prayed over this tragic news. The king noticed that his cheerful cupbearer was sad, and he said, "This is nothing but sorrow of heart." In another place of the Bible we read, "By sorrow of the heart the spirit is broken." But it is also true that "A merry heart maketh a cheerful countenance" (Prov. 15:13).

Now we must hasten to fill the prescription that is given to make the heart strong: "Wait on the Lord; be of good courage, and he shall strengthen thine heart: wait, I say, on the Lord" (Ps. 27:14). We cannot be burdened with care and expect to have abounding health. Cast "all your care upon him, for he careth for you" (I Peter 5:7). This faith and confidence in the Lord will benefit you more than regular visits to your physician, or doctoring with pills and poultices. "A merry heart doeth good like a medicine" (Prov. 17:22). Trusting the Lord is a good habit of mind. It will brighten your smile and give wings to your troubles. "And the peace of God, which passeth all understanding, shall keep your hearts and minds through Christ Jesus" (Phil. 4:7). We see that faith and confidence become a stabilizing power in our daily life, and this verse will be fulfilled: "Be of good courage, and he shall strengthen your heart, all ye that hope in the Lord" (Ps. 31:24).

A Christian Wrestling

Let not mine enemies triumph over me.—Psalm 25:2

LET US LOOK INTO the New Testament to find the wrestling that we, as children of God, will have to engage in. Ours is as tough or a tougher assignment than Jacob's. It is a daily conflict. We must "be strong in the Lord and in the power of his might" if we are to be winners. We meet our opponent head-on. If we fall down on the *mat* of circumstances, we will be overcome. God tells us to "stand" and "withstand." To "withstand" implies aggressive wrestling. If we are to keep our footing, we must stand in the power of His might. "When I said, my foot slippeth; thy mercy, O Lord, held me up" (Ps. 94:18). We battle a powerful antagonist, but we have a Great Coach. Jesus our wonderful Lord is by our side to train us and prepare us for life's sharpest conflicts. He has promised the wrestler "though he fall, he shall not be utterly cast down; for the Lord upholdeth him with his hand" (Ps. 37:24). What equipment He has provided, too! Read about it in Ephesians 6:10-18.

Family worship is the time and place to learn about this wrestling. "Your adversary the devil goeth about as a roaring lion seeking whom he may devour"; "We wrestle not against flesh and blood, but against spiritual wickedness in high places" (I Peter 5:8; Eph. 6:12).

Wrestlers need courage and tenacity of purpose. We *must* win over our adversary. He never will be the victor if we don the armor that is provided for us.

102

"Wherefore take unto you the whole armor of God, that ye may be able to withstand in the evil day, and having done all, to stand."

To belong to God's winning team, mothers, we must have steadfastness of purpose. Rearing our boys and girls for the Lord challenges all the ability God has bestowed upon us. God will honor our earnest efforts. Ask Him to re-enforce the resolves you have made for Him.

We are urged "to fight the good fight of faith." The wrestling we mothers do actually demands strength "in the inner man." Even our nerves are sometimes strained in a conflict. We need fortitude to withstand temptations and testings. You see that it is a single-handed combat. There is no place to give up in despair or to lose by default. When you encounter an apparently unconquerable foe, take this predicament to the Lord in prayer. "Is anything too hard for the Lord?" Tell Him all about your heartaches and struggles. You will have the joy of beholding Him alleviate your most difficult situations. Each time you come out victor, your faith will be stronger for the next engagement with the enemy.

Sometimes when we have mental conflict, we feel exhausted physically. We have exerted so much energy and determination in making a momentous decision that we become exhausted. Often this struggle involves the choice between the right and the wrong path. You know what is right, but you are tempted to do wrong. The decision of the particular wrestling match is hanging in the balance. One more *hold* and the devil will get you down. Hasten and put on the whole armor of God—"be strong in the Lord."

You will be saved a humiliating defeat. You will never regret choosing righteousness rather than wickedness. "For whatsoever a man soweth, that shall he also reap" (Gal. 6:7). You have to be desperately determined in order to wrestle successfully against spiritual wickedness and sin.

Other times the decision we must make is a matter of expediency. This does not involve a moral issue, but a choice. Perhaps a lifework is at stake. What would be the wisest and best course to pursue? You have come to a crossroads, and one way may prove to be a detour. The Lord has the wrestling schedule all planned for your life, so take this problem to Him in prayer also.

Problems of conduct are your own personal responsibility. No one can settle them for you. You cannot side-step the issues. They cannot be postponed. You must contend, resist, withstand shortcomings and weaknesses. Either you will stand "in the strength of the Lord," or you will be overcome by temptation and then you will sin. Even partial defeat leaves you weaker in character for the next onslaught.

Contemplation of the strength of our foe disarms us and causes us to tremble. Still the neon sign of encouragement shines from the pages of the Bible: "Nay in all these things we are more than conquerors through him that loved us" (Rom. 8:37).

What are some of these problems we must wrestle with? Here are a few of them: struggling to overcome a bad habit; longing to improve an unlovely disposition; restraining complaint against unfavorable circumstances and surroundings; overcoming frequent misunderstandings with one member of the household; facing a baffling discipline problem; conquering a harmful tendency to be partial to one child and harsh to another; struggling against selfishness in the fair budgeting of the family's meager income; curbing unwise expenditures.

Four times in this scripture we are told to *"stand."* We will not falter, we will not sink to our knees in terror or dismay. We will look to Jesus. We will be strong "in the Lord and in the power of his might." "He is my defense, I shall not be greatly moved" (Ps. 62:2). We are trusting our Saviour to renew and increase our militant purpose.

"By this I know that thou favorest me, because mine enemy doth not triumph over me" (Ps. 41:11).

Workers Together — Husband and Wife

Being heirs together of the grace of life.—I Peter 3:7

THE HAPPINESS AND PEACE of a home are established on the congenial relationship existing between a husband and wife.

Our minds go back to days of courtship. First there came that slow realization and thrilling awakening that someone cared for you only. There had been other admirers, but this time you met the one who truly understood you and loved you. Your heart responded with equal love and devotion. To both of you there seemed to be only two people in the world—you and your lover. Sometimes you talked excitedly about the future. Other times there was an understanding silence between you. It was all so restful and joyous.

Then we relive the wedding day, with vows and promises so solemnly uttered. Now at last we are on our own. We belong to each other forever, united in Christ. Our Christian aims and purposes will vitalize our new venture.

This idea of love and homemaking originated in Heaven. It is God's plan for earthly happiness. Home should be the most enjoyable place in the world for both husband and wife. It is a haven of refuge from greed and selfishness. It is a retreat for the renewal of physical strength and mental alertness. It is the best place to relax. We can be our own happy selves in our very own home.

"Husbands, love your wives and be not bitter

against them." In the stress and strain of business, bitterness may creep into a home. We must pray against it. Often the wife has labored all day long, only to be met in the evening by her husband wearing a frown and uttering a snarl. He loves her deeply, yet he is surly. Thoughtlessly we hurt those we love the most.

The years have gone by so fast. There are children in the house. Sometimes it is hard to believe that they belong to us. We are overwhelmed to think that the Lord would give us such fine, healthy, vigorous youngsters. Again we are appalled to see so many of our own characteristics so distinctly displayed by our sons and daughters.

How marvelous is God's creation! We will never cease marveling at the birth of a little babe. The creation of every human being is indeed a miracle.

"And the wife see that she reverence her husband." Do you reverence your husband? Do you have implicit faith in his judgment? Do you hold him up to your children as a man to be respected? Or do you ridicule him in front of his children? Do you belittle his advice and laugh at his schemes?

A wife is the silent partner in her husband's business success. It will never be known how much a man's success is due to his wife's confidence in him. Her shrewd foresight has been sound and helpful. Few men will attribute their success to their wives. Some do give them credit for wise judgment in business affairs.

One man has been so much more successful than other men. Is this success due in some measure at least to the "reverence" his wife has shown him? That is the scriptural program. "Her husband is known in the gates when he sitteth among the elders of the land." He has won a place of honor in the community, and his wife had a large share in the winning of it.

Recall again those first days of romance. Renew your love and respect for your husband. Your reliance on him will send him forth with the assurance that he can conquer.

God has ordained that the man should be the head of his house. Many women resent this plan. Actually it is one of the finest arrangements for their peace of mind. Why take the burden of the household on your shoulders? Leave it where it belongs. Trust the responsibility of major issues to your husband. This dependence will be a continual source of restfulness to you. It will re-enforce your conviction that you chose wisely when you married such a capable man.

These attitudes of a mother are sensed by the children. They will love and respect their father if their mother loves him. Their keen perception will also reflect your faith and confidence in "Dad." Reverence for your husband is your love in action.

Make your home a shelter *from* the terrific storms of life. Some women make it a "storm center."

Contradicting each other before the children will confuse them. They will not know whom to obey.

Wordy opposition between parents is deplorable. If you have differences of opinion, wait until you are alone to talk them over and smooth them out. Contention will divide your home and affect your children's sense of security.

Live a victorious Christian life together. Thank the Lord for His explicit directions for a happy marriage. United in purpose, you will cause your home to stand. Divided in viewpoint, you will both fail. Meet together at the family altar.

> Christ is the head of this home,
> The unseen guest at every meal,
> The silent listener to every conversation.

Daily Thanks-living— Labors of Love

Show forth his salvation from day to day.
—Psalm 96:2

THE GIVING OF THANKS should be an everyday occurrence. The spirit of thanksgiving should linger in the heart throughout the year.

"It is a good thing to give thanks unto the Lord, and to sing praises unto thy name, O most high; to show forth thy lovingkindness in the morning, and thy faithfulness every night" (Ps. 92:1, 2). This is a wonderfully comprehensive program for a Christian mother. In the morning, speak of God's lovingkindness, and talk about His faithfulness every night.

How did you get along this morning before the family went off for the day? Was there a happy rushing hither and thither? Was there the usual search for overshoes, lost tickets, or a misplaced glove? Was everyone shouting at everyone else? Was there a general atmosphere of tension? Christian patience is the antidote for these difficulties. God has planned the home to be a place of joy and thanksgiving.

One of the first rules for a tranquil send-off in the morning is to rise early enough so that there will be time for an unhurried breakfast. Extra time should be allowed on rainy mornings, to button up the raincoats and put on rubbers, a bit more time in cold or wintry weather.

Perhaps you already realize it, Mother, but you are the one who gives the musical pitch and unconsciously selects the melody for the day. Your note of thanksgiving to start the day may echo in the hearts of your family until eventide. Pray and strive to maintain a home of happy harmonies. This tone of thanksgiving will then be an integral part of your family life. In contrast to this cheerful tune, mothers may begin the day with a doleful note in a minor key.

Your family straggles back one by one in the evening. They may be cold and hungry. Each in turn closes the door on the outside world and calls, "I'm home." Is this a signal for rejoicing on your part, or do you meet the incoming members with a sigh, a scowl and complaints? "And be ye thankful." You can make each supper meal a banquet. You, Mother, can direct the conversation into happy channels. You will succeed in making everyone happy at the table, and the meal will be a feast of good things. "He that is of a merry heart hath a continual feast."

The habit of giving God thanks for the food at mealtime is an example of thanksgiving in action. It would be torture to hear your child cry for bread and be unable to satisfy his need. If you have not done it, start now to thank the Lord for the abundance of food He has provided. Your entire dependence is upon Him. "Be thankful unto him, and bless his name. Show forth his salvation from day to day" (Ps. 100:4; 96:2).

Have you ever watched the customers milling through a chain grocery store? Five o'clock comes and the stream of buyers increases. After the cash register has rung up a thousand dollars' worth of sales, the shelves are still well-stocked. There is a surplus in all "our barns and storehouses, in our granaries and silos." Do we thank God for this plenty?

Let us choose for our thanksgiving verse, "My cup runneth over." When you are tempted to complain, look up to the Lord and say, "My cup runneth over." The Bible uses superlatives in describing what the Christian has: abounding, everlasting, boundless, full, inexhaustible, good measure, shaken down and running over, and showers of blessing. Does all this overwhelming provision strike a thankful chord in

111

your heart? "What can I render unto the Lord for all his benefits? I will take the cup of salvation and call upon the name of the Lord" (Ps. 116:2).

Your cup of salvation is continually running over with blessing. "So great salvation" is the root of your thanksgiving. This in turn flowers into praise and adoration daily. "Blessed be the Lord who daily loadeth us with benefits, even the God of our salvation" (Ps. 68:19). And so the Holy Spirit outpouring in your heart overflows into the lives of your husband and children. This spirit of thanksgiving can be a soprano obligato. It will be a melody of praise accompanying all your daily labors of love for your family. "So we thy people and sheep of thy pasture will give thee thanks forever; we will show forth thy praise to all generations" (Ps. 79:13).

The Teen-Ager

Remember now thy Creator in the days of thy youth.—Ecclesiastes 12:1

YOUR CHILDREN ARE GROWING up and soon the oldest will become a teen-ager. Instead of dreading adolescence with its adjustments, anticipate it with real pleasure. Although the teen-ager doesn't know as much as he thinks he does, he will surprise you with his originality. Be on the lookout for these trends. Youthful approaches to problems are amusing and different. Remember there are many views of a single landscape. His keen insight often simplifies an otherwise tough problem.

Children keep a mother's opinions elastic and pliable. She will never be set in her ways as long as there are children in her home. Versatility comes often because of the stress of family life. Sometimes it is a question who is getting the most discipline, the mother or the child. Self-control, patience, and love must triumph in a mother's life, else the battle will be lost.

Every growing youngster experiences unhappy and grumpy moods. A peevish mood is very unpleasant while it lasts. Be gentle and patient with that child of yours. Someone has said that all that can be done with a boy at these tempestuous times is "to love him and feed him." He is growing taller fast. Mark his height on the room wall and notice his gain in stature. This rapid growth is the cause of his irritability. With this added strength he will soar into young manhood.

Teen-agers love to be on the go day and night, without restriction. Here is your chance to score, Mother. You can be the one fixed quantity in their otherwise turbulent existence. Home can be a sweet retreat from the world. Here they find a devoted mother they can always rely on.

When dinnertime comes around, your boy will remember that mother is ready and waiting. He will picture the steaming hot meal and his empty chair at the family table. Your regularity and promptness will have a stabilizing effect on your restless son. He knows his mother is expecting him, and he is constrained to hurry home. She'll be looking for him to poke his head in at the kitchen door. Her cheery greeting will repay his promptness.

Any hour of the night Mother is still waiting. No matter how quietly the front door opens, the key grinds too loudly in the lock and the door hinges squeak. Mother never seems to be asleep. The teenager sighs with the futility of trying to get in noiselessly. Mother whispers to him, then hears a word or two about the evening. She may press a kiss on his forehead. He is convinced once again of his mother's continual care of him.

Do you have a teen-ager in *your* family? Have you discovered that their judgments and conclusions are very immature? Young people are impulsive and often unreasonably sensitive. A trivial remark will irritate and anger them. They resent advice and rebel against instruction. The situation sometimes reaches the stage where the parent is regarded as a "mossback" and the teen-ager sincerely believes he knows the right and only answers. The parents, being aware of this attitude, can lay their plans for strategy, advance, and victory. The father may be unable to give this turn of affairs the necessary supervision, so it then becomes the mother's problem.

During these trying years of rapid growth, avoid being dictatorial and dogmatic. If you are dictatorial you will lose your youngster's confidence, affection, and loyalty. Coercion and severity will build up an impassable barrier between you. His attitude will be defiant. His response will be one of resentment and condemnation.

Motherhood is a full-time job. Maternal efficiency can rightfully expect an abundant payoff. A Christian mother sows the Word of God faithfully each morning at family worship, and her pay envelope is delivered after years of prayerful labor.

Try the tactful approach. Give your child the opportunity to make his own decisions. This will strengthen his character. Match his impatience with your patience. Ignore his impudence. Pray for his adjustments and friendships. Encourage him in his ambitions. Listen to his dreams. He'll unload them if you give him a chance. Expressing his ideals helps to crystallize them. Later he will realize these high aspirations. Share his hopes and love affairs. You will never forfeit your control by this companionable method.

The Book of Proverbs is bulging with wise advice for the teen-ager.

The Timid Child

That we may be able to comfort them which are in any trouble.—II Corinthians 1:4

ONE OF YOUR CHILDREN may be especially timid. Does his bashfulness annoy and embarrass you? Be assured that your shy child is suffering more than you are. Some mothers scold their defenseless child publicly. "I'd be ashamed of myself," the mother says; and with a push she adds, "Get in there and have a good time with the other boys and girls." The child acts like a balky colt and stubbornly resists this coercion. It is a mistake to drive a bashful boy or girl. The use of force usually ends in a drawn battle with neither the mother nor the child winning a decision. Some of us can remember our own timidity.

First, you must evidence love toward your bashful child, even when he embarrasses you by his silence and unresponsiveness. You are his one refuge. Don't deprive him of that needed shelter and security. An understanding mother will enfold such a child in her love. Coping with timidity is your immediate problem. You can accept it grudgingly as a distasteful task, or it can become an absorbing challenge.

Your objective envisions the happiness and well-being of your child. Gentleness is one of your principal weapons.

David started as a modest shepherd boy. He became a brave, fearless soldier and a wise king. God had dealt gently with him and he exclaimed, "Thy gentleness hath made me great." Our maternal care should be equally gentle. Tender care will inspire your child, likewise, to do exploits. Many biographies of famous men have been dedicated to mothers whose unforgettable source of power sprang from their gentleness.

A timid child has a sensitive nature. His timidity is intensified by harsh discipline. Rather than offend his parents, he suppresses even his rightful longings and desires. He shrinks from controversy in the family circle. He prefers to tell his secrets to his pets for they give him a sympathetic hearing!

School days are difficult for a retiring, timid child. The boys and girls at play dart here and there in the schoolyard and he feels miserably alone. If he does play, he dreads the possibility of making an error or losing the game for his side.

Parties are torture for a shy child. His silence is painful. His comments are often pointless and ill-timed. The other young guests either ridicule his remarks as foolish or ignore his pleasantries as uninteresting and boring. Don't force him to go to the birthday party if he doesn't want to go. Discuss with him the purchase of an appropriate gift. Every child has a standard of value. A cheap gift would increase his embarrassment. Wrap up the well-chosen gift with gay paper and ribbon. With these preliminaries you may find your child more willing to go to the party.

A timid child may be restless and nervous. Help him find a place of happy usefulness. Mother, this is your opportunity to step into the picture with all the wisdom and tact that God has given you. A hobby may appeal to this type of child. The interest of a special craft will engross him. His self-consciousness will be forgotten in new explorations and discoveries.

You need divine guidance to deal successfully with your bashful child. Earthly wisdom and child psychology avail little. "But the wisdom that is from above is first pure, then peaceable, gentle, and easy to be entreated, full of mercy and good fruits, without partiality, and without hypocrisy" (James 3:17). Gentleness is one of these "good fruits" of the Holy Spirit that should glow in a mother's heart.

Many of us adults are timid children of God. We are restless and know not which way to turn. Hear Christ's gentle invitation: "Come unto me, all ye that labor and are heavy laden." This divine provision appeals to all of us for we are a laboring people and often very weary. To our ready response He adds this gentle promise, "And I will give you rest."

"Like as a father pitieth his children, so the Lord pitieth them that fear him" (Ps. 103:13).

Jittery Wives

That your joy may be full.--John 15:11

THESE THOUGHTS ARE ESPECIALLY beamed to nervous wives and jittery young mothers. Maybe you are restless and discontented, and your expression is not a happy one. You seem to be preoccupied

118

and burdened with unsolved problems. Perhaps you have forgotten that Bible verse, "Be anxious for *nothing,* but in everything by prayer and supplication with thanksgiving, let your requests be made known unto God" (Phil. 4:6, 7). Some mothers live in a "worry world."

Your days with your young family should be among the happiest of your life. There are many word pictures in the Bible that portray various scenes of the home and married life. In the very first reference to Adam and Eve we are told that God created Eve as a help meet for Adam. Then the Scripture adds, "And he brought her unto the man." This was the beginning of the first home. (Let this incident assure Christian young people that the partner the Lord brings to them will be a suitable life partner.)

Again in the Bible it is written, "A man taketh unto himself a wife." The man is the aggressor in deciding to marry and establish a home. This is the divine order. He is voluntarily shouldering the responsibility of this difficult and uncertain task. No marriage vow was ever uttered that did not involve suffering as well as joy. "Man is born to trouble as the sparks fly upward." In the following verse we see the man again taking the initiative. "Whoso findeth a wife findeth a good thing, and obtaineth favor of the Lord" (Prov. 18:22). He looked for a helpmate. His search was successful.

Many women reverse this Biblical order so that it

reads incorrectly, "A wife taketh unto herself a husband." They have actually taken upon their own weak and inadequate shoulders an impossible task. They have unnecessarily assumed the support and guidance of a particular man as well as the direction of their future together. The husbands are faithful workers, but they refuse to enjoy their diligence. No woman should suffer this added anxiety either physically or mentally. God never intended that she should. She may break under the strain.

Worried mothers may sit down and list a mother's assets. The best way to solve a weighty problem is to bring it out into the open, analyze it and find its spiritual solution. "For God hath not given us the spirit of fear; but of power, and of love, and of a sound mind" (II Tim. 1:7).

Your first asset is one strong husband. Thank the Lord he is capable and God has made him that way. His shoulders are broad and he is somewhat immune to the opinons of others. His feelings are not easily hurt. He is efficient; if there is a chore around the house, he does it well. If it is a job for his employer, he does it faithfully. I say again, thank God for such a husband.

Instead of worrying about the burden of living, just relax and let your husband lead. *Enjoy* being a follower. It will rebuild your frazzled nerves. Before you were married, you had to be alert and aggressive to earn your living. Pushing and forging ahead became a habit to you. Now it is hard to stay quietly at home and watch your husband battle the world. Ask the Lord to help you appreciate the luxury of sitting on the sidelines. Let your partner do the exploits for a change. If you carry his burden of earning a living, you will make him as nervous as you are yourself. Remember, "The peace of God will guard and keep your hearts and minds in Christ Jesus."

One of the compensations of marriage is companionship. It is good to have each other to depend on. The cold world of outsiders misjudges, mistreats, and falsely condemns you. You have each other for mutual consolation and courage. You may be solitary, but never lonely. Together you can "watch the rest of the world go by." As long as you have each other, there need never be a bleak season in your lives. The years will pile up. The autumn will extend into Indian summer. There will be warm pleasant days with orange and gold colorings long after the last child has left home. What joy to be heirs together of the grace of life!

What does the nervous wife and mother need most? She needs peace and quiet faith. Here is her promise, "Thou wilt keep him in perfect peace whose mind is stayed on thee, because he trusteth in thee" (Isa. 26:3). Our Saviour understands best the individual's need. "Peace I leave with you, my peace I give unto you: not as the world giveth give I unto you. Let not your heart be troubled, neither let it be afraid" (John 14:27). Are you casting all your care upon Him because He careth for you?

"Live joyfully with the . . . youth whom thou lovest, all the days of thy life" (Eccles. 9:9). Not exactly the verse given, but certainly its advice works for women as well.

Taste and Flavor

Salt is good.—Mark 9:50

REMEMBER THE DINNER YOU planned and cooked with such care? Everyone was looking forward to the meal with mouth-watering anticipation. When Dad and the children were seated at the table, you carried in the steaming hot dish with pardonable pride. Dad said Mother was always doing such nice things. With this praise, he dished out large helpings. The first taste brought forth groans. You had forgotten the salt! By the time you rushed to the kitchen and stirred in the missing ingredient, the appearance of the food was sadly changed. Of course, mothers do not cry, but sometimes they feel like it.

Job asked, "Can that which is unsavory be eaten without salt? Or is there any taste in the white of an egg?"

Salt gives flavor to all foods. It is the one staple in this day of inflation that has not gone up in price. The round blue boxes are piled high in the grocery store. The price tag on the edge of the shelf is unchanged.

Salt has always been indispensable. We must eat it to live. Our forefathers learned the value of salt when they were deprived of it and needed it desperately. Do you remember reading of the time in American history when salt was taxed unmercifully? Salt is often mentioned in the Bible. In Old Testament times no sacrifice was acceptable to God without salt. Tons of salt must have been available for the countless sacrifices which were offered. "And every oblation of thy meat offering shalt thou season with salt; neither shalt thou suffer the salt of the covenant of thy God to be lacking from thy meat offering: with all thine offerings thou shalt offer salt" (Lev. 2:13).

Salt has many valuable uses. Christians, like salt, are essential in this tasteless, insipid world. Christ said to those who believed and followed Him, "Ye are the salt of the earth." The love of Christ in our hearts energizes us to care for the aged and to shelter the orphans and widows. Christ's love flavors and stimulates these acts of thoughtfulness. It heightens our concern for the helpless and needy.

Missionaries in all parts of the earth carry this loving care into heathen lands. There the elderly people and little children are forlorn and destitute. Our vanquished foes and our captured enemies are treated with kindness instead of being killed or tortured. It is because we have a Christian heritage that we are feeding many peoples today.

123

All food tastes flat and uninteresting without salt. Salt gives savor to food. Just so, Christians give savor to living. How monotonous would be our existence if we worked only to buy food, and then ate it in order to work some more! Such a life would be tiresome and without objective. How does the Christian add spice and savor to this dreary round? In the first place the Christian's eyes are on eternity rather than on time. Heaven is the utimate goal. We are keenly anticipating the day when we shall see our Saviour face to face. This hope keeps the Christan sweet. Like salt, it has a preserving effect. "And I pray God your whole spirit and soul and body be preserved blameless unto the coming of our Lord Jesus Christ. Faithful is he that calleth you who also will do it" (I Thess. 5:23).

Salt loses some of its strength when it is impure. It becomes white and sparkling when it is purified. The Christian must likewise be pure if he is to be the salt of the earth. "But if the salt have lost its savor, wherewith shall it be salted? It is henceforth good for nothing, but to be cast out and to be trodden under foot of men" (Matt. 5:13).

Purity of word and action will overflow from a pure heart. "Let your speech be alway with grace seasoned with salt." Are you gracious and kind in all you say? Is your presence in your family and among your friends an influence for good? Are you a tower of strength and help because, like salt, you are most necessary? The Lord Jesus wants to make lives that are pure and sparkling in this impure old world.

Pictures in Little and Youthful Minds

When I remember these things, I pour out my soul in me.—Psalm 42:4

THE MIND IS AN ART gallery of memories. There are glad pictures and sad pictures. We have forgotten many incidents and small tragedies of our childhood, but certain happenings are indelibly stamped on our minds. Some childhood scenes are so clearly etched in our memories that we can re-live them in minute detail.

The smell of meat broth simmering on the electric stove reminds one of the old coal range in the big kitchen. Washday was always a tiring day for Mother. The top of the stove would be covered with heavy flatirons. They were being heated for afternoon work at the ironing board. The family washing and ironing were all crowded into one day. Of course, there was little time for cooking, but appetites knew no vacation; so Mother would plan beef broth with macaroni and vegetables. No one ever heard of vitamins in those days, though of course they were just as important and necessary as now. It must have been God who gave Mother the wisdom to serve this well-balanced meal. These were the days before modern linoleum; there was no covering on the spotless wooden floor of the kitchen.

Or, I can see again the picture that hung for years on the wall of my little bedroom. In the fading twilight I watched the sad little girl who spilled her milk at the lunch table. The same framed picture met my gaze when I opened my eyes each bright new morning. Forty years have passed, but the little girl never stopped crying and the milk continues to drip from the clean white tablecloth to the carpeted floor.

There are pictures which never have been painted on canvas, but are equally vivid. You remember the lighthearted and happy feeling you experienced when your teacher smiled at you with approval. The sad memory remains when you were so selfish and stingy with a bag of birthday chocolates. Perhaps your visit to a beautiful farm flashes across your memory. You especially remember the big work horse you patted ever so cautiously.

Did you have a grandmother whose restful expression proclaimed her inner peace with God? You can see her sitting in her little rocking chair as clearly as she sat years ago. Do you have "the joy of the Lord" in your heart, as she did? "When I call to remembrance the unfeigned faith which is in thee which dwelt first in thy grandmother Lois and thy mother Eunice, and I am persuaded in thee also." What a precious picture of the past! Everyone and everything has changed sharply through the years, but the memories remain the same.

The baby starts storing away pictures in his little mind at a surprisingly early age. His parents are a sweet refuge from all danger. Mother's skirts are such a safe hiding place. Daddy's arms are the strongest and the best in his little world. Indelible impressions increase with the years. How important that you plan each day a store of happy memories for your children! It is picture-taking time, in young lives. The finished pictures will be theirs for life.

Stow away the memory of *happy* Sundays spent in Sunday school and church. Make Sunday school a habit. A child is especially responsive to a regular schedule. Daily prayer will make a lasting impression on his precious life. Ask God to enable you to deal wisely with the delicate films of little minds.

May your children remember you as a godly mother, one who knelt beside the little bed at night to talk confidentially with the Lord Jesus about them. May they know God better because together you thank Him for the food at mealtime. May you take them to the throne of grace at family worship time. How lovingly those children of long ago must have remembered that happy day when the Lord Jesus "took them up in his arms, put his hands upon them and blessed them"! He still pleads: "Suffer the little children to come unto me, and *forbid them not.*"

Every fond childhood memory can be intertwined

with trust and faith in our wonderful Saviour. "Thou shalt remember all the way which the Lord thy God led thee" (Deut. 8:2).